AF608214

CATHOLIC UNIVERSITY OF AMERICA
STUDIES IN CANON LAW
No. 50

The Third Order Secular of St. Francis

A DISSERTATION

SUBMITTED TO THE FACULTY OF CANON LAW OF THE CATHOLIC UNIVERSITY OF AMERICA IN PARTIAL FULFILLMENT OF THE REQUIREMENTS FOR THE DEGREE OF DOCTOR IN CANON LAW

BY

GERALD JOSEPH REINMANN, J. C. L.,

Priest of the Order of Friars Minor Conventual,
Province of the Immaculate Conception,
Syracuse, N. Y.

CATHOLIC UNIVERSITY OF AMERICA
WASHINGTON, D. C.
1928

IMPRIMI POTEST:

Ferdinandus Mayer, O. M. C.

Minister Provincialis

Syracusis in N. E., die 4 Junii, 1928

NIHIL OBSTAT:

✠ Thomas J. Shahan, S. T. D., J. U. D.

Censor Deputatus

Washingtonii, D. C., die 25 Maii, 1928

IMPRIMATUR:

✠ Michael J. Curley

Archiepiscopus Baltimorensis

Baltimorae, die Maii, 1928

(Printed in U. S. A.)

FOREWORD

The Third Order Secular of St. Francis is a society which has been favored and urged forward by the Holy See perhaps more than any other lay association. Many of the recent Pontiffs have declared that it is *the* institution upon which the Church bases her hope of general salvation, because its principles are so conducive to law and order not only in reference to the spiritual, but to the temporal and civil as well. It was with this thought in view that Leo XIII declared that 'my social reform is the Third Order of St. Francis.'

Several canonical treatises on this institution of the Church have already been written. The purpose of the present work is to explain more in detail the various papal pronouncements on this wide-spread institution of the Catholic Church, and thus to give a more comprehensive idea of its organization and government in conformity with the great number of decrees which have emanated from the Holy See, as well as with the present Code of Canon Law.

The legislation in regard to the Third Order was changed very little by the Code: hence it is to be hoped that the numerous citations of papal *decrees,* rather than canons, will not convey the impression that too much latitude has been given to the historical side of the question, even in the part which treats of the present canonical legislation.

The definition and purpose of the Order has been treated in the canonical part, with the thought in view that the reader will have gained a comprehensive idea of this by a perusal of the historical development of the institution. The original Rule of the Order, or, the *Regula Antiqua*—as well as the *Rule of Leo XIII*—are given *in extenso* in the appendix, in order that a ready reference may be had to the citations. Italics, unless otherwise stated, are to be considered those of the present writer.

TABLE OF CONTENTS

APPENDIX OF RULES OF THE ORDER

PART 1

The Historico canonical Development of the Third Order Secular

Authors agree that the monks of St. Benedict were the forerunners, if indeed they were not the first, to propagate the idea of the laity being in some manner connected with the monasteries and abbeys of the religious, both in a spiritual and material manner. Any great organization is not momentarily conceived and immediately put into effect as a *successful* culmination of that idea. It is rather the effect of time and the previous experience of years that have always influenced great movements and trends in the various institutes of the Catholic Church. There is no doubt that St. Francis was the first to organize completely and successfully to accomplish the union of the secular with the religious, the feasibility of a religious life in the world, with rules that at the same time allow the continuance of family life and its necessary contact with the world. "What till then no founder of a religious order had thought of—to make the religious life common property—he [Francis] was the first to devise and, by God's favor, to successfully accomplish * * *".[1]

But at the same time it must be admitted that the great monastic leaders—forerunners of St. Francis—planted the seed which he later cultivated and brought into full bloom

[1]Benedict XV, const. *Sacra propediem,* Jan. 6, 1921 (*A. A. S.* [1921], XIII, 34).

under the able guidance and leadership of Cardinal Ugolino who later became Pope Gregory IX.[3]

Therefore a brief history of the various lay associations which preceded the Third Order Secular of St. Francis will give a better understanding of its foundation and government.

CHAPTER I

The Secular Oblates of St. Benedict

The name *oblate* in its strict sense signifies that which is offered or brought. In the early days of monasticism young children were brought to the abbeys and offered to the service in much the same manner as the first-born in the Old Testament. In the Rule of St. Benedict there is a provision made for parents to bring their child to the monastery with an offering and they were obliged to 'make a written document and swear under oath never to give him anything or the means to acquire anything; or if they are unwilling to do this then let them make an oblation to the monastery and they can receive the income thereof during their life.'[4]

Besides the cloistered oblates and monks who lived a com-

[3]"In quo egregiam ei operam navavit, ut accepimus, Cardinalis Ugolinus, is qui deinde, Gregorii IX sibi imposito nomine * * *" (*o. c.*, 35); cf. Cocchi, *Commentarium*, IV, n. 185; Chelodi, *Jus de Personis*, n. 302; that the monastic forerunners of St. Francis, especially the Benedictines, exerted influence on the foundation of the Third Order Secular of St. Francis is also affirmed by: Prümmer, *Manuale Juris Canonici*, Q. 270; Thurston, "Scapulars", *The Month* [1927], CXLIX, p 484 f; Augustine, *A Commentary,* III, p 443 f; concerning the influence of the Humiliates on the Franciscan Third Order, cf. *A. F. H.*, VI, p 173 f; a complete treatise on this subject is given by Van Den Borne, *Die Anfänge des Franziskanischen Dritten Ordens (Franziskanische Studien,* Beiheft VIII).

[4]Butler, *Regula Monastica,* chap. IV, 105.

munity life at an abbey under the obedience of an abbot, there was a custom among pious Christians of offering themselves and their goods to the monastery and then to remain at home; married people also lived at home but according to the Rule of the Order. This happened not only among the Benedictines themselves, but also among the various branches of the Benedictine Order. Already at the time of St. Benedict and Maurus such persons formed themselves into a brotherhood with the order. As the Benedictine Order spread, many of the laity desired to have some connection with it in order to acquire a brotherhood with the monks and to be the adopted children of St. Benedict.[4]

The institute of Oblates received its development in the monasteries of Hirschau in the eleventh century; but the real origin was not in these places and historical documents available do not give sufficient matter to establish this in an exact manner. There was no fixed order in the beginning: the monks, retired from the world, could not prepare themselves for their relations with it which later became necessary. Their liturgy and influence were not sufficiently developed to assure them of social influence. But after the invasion by the barbarians the Church demanded that they should take to the conquest of new peoples, and by their preaching subdue them to the yoke of the Gospel. Kings and princes made it a point of honor to multiply the centers of monastic life; cities really formed around the monasteries and the inhabitants cultivated the monastic domains.[5]

Mabillon says that the Benedictine Rule admitted in principle indistinctly children and adults, youths, poor as well as rich, nobles as well as common people, serfs as well as

[4]Beringer, *Die Ablässe,* II, n. 409; cf. Heimbucher, *Die Orden und Kongregationen der Katholischen Kirche,* I, p 271.

[5]"Les Oblats", *Revue Benedictine,* III [1886-1887], p 58.

free, learned as well as the ignorant, the laity as well as the clergy.[6]

The Rule of St. Fructus, chapter six, bears this title: "How men can live without peril in a monastery with their wives and children." Then the Rule goes on to state that when a married couple present themselves to the abbot they are to submit to his authority, and can have no more clothing than necessary. The parents should instruct their children in the Rule and are not to speak to them unnecessarily.[7]

Another institution of the Benedictines was that of virgins and widows who were consecrated to God but lived with their families.[8]

Again there are many instances of families retiring near a monastery and making a donation of their goods to the abbey, for which in return they received their sustenance and a share in the prayers and good works of the monks. As early as 817 St. Benedict of Aniane attempted in the following words to put an end to the custom of allowing laity and clerics in the monasteries: "Laity and clerics are not allowed to be received into the monastery unless they wish to become monks"; however, it seems that this admonition was not generally observed.[9] Although this may have been an abuse, it nevertheless proves the desire of people in the world to be connected in some manner with the religious life.

That the laity were allowed to live *near* the abbeys can be seen from the records of the ninth century, in which Wildebald is described as giving his goods to the monastery and being employed to care for travelers. As a condition of his donation, he demanded to live in the guest house and to

[6]*O. c.*, 59.

[7]Migne, *P. L.*, LXXXVII, 1115 f.

[8]"Les Oblats", *o. c.*, p 109.

[9]This prohibition was made at the Synod of Aixle Chapelle ("Les Oblats", *o. c.*, p 107).

receive food and clothing for the remainder of his life.[10]

The early oblates may be grouped into four classes:

1st class: Laity who pledged themselves to the service of the monastery and lived near it after promising obedience to the abbot.

2nd class: Seculars who served the monasteries although remaining with their families and retaining ownership of their goods on condition of giving an annual sum to the monastery. It appears that this sacrifice was made in order to be near the monastery, to share in its merits, to help with the prayers and to be under the influence of the monks.

3rd class: Persons who made a donation of their goods to the monastery and received their subsistence either at the abbey itself or in their own homes.

4th class: Those who made a donation of their goods to the monks, but received them back by a new title of benefice, of which they reserved to themselves the use and usufruct.[11]

At the end of the twelfth century, the third class at the monastery of Admont was composed of a number of 'fratres obedientiarii,' i. e. a group of lay people who voluntarily submitted themselves to the service of the religious without any monastic profession.[12] Some classes bound themselves more strictly than others.[13] At times women would retire near a monastery, assist in the making of sacred vestments, and the care of the poor *at their own expense;*[14] hence the vow of poverty was certainly not embraced by this class.

This short history conveys at least some idea of the tendency on the part of the laity from early monastic times, to

[10] *Ibidem*, p 108.

[11] *Ibidem*, p 159; Du Cange, *Glossarium ad Scriptores*, s. v. Oblati, Donati.

[12] "Les Oblats", *o. c.*, p 209 f.

[13] Cf. Migne, *P. L.*, CXLIII, 347.

[14] "Les Oblats", *o. c.*, p 216.

connect themselves in some manner with the religious life in order to derive spiritual benefit. The Abbeys of Monte Cassino and Subiaco possessed this institution in the fourteenth and fifteenth centuries and have since perpetuated it. But due to the fact that the Rules and the manner of receiving Oblates had varied according to time and place, the General Chapter of the Benedictine Order in 1590 desired new regulations, which were subsequently edited and printed at Palermo in 1628. These Rules were then made obligatory in the various abbeys and have been the groundword for all subsequent editions.[18]

The following is a summary of their contents:

1. The Oblates are God-fearing Christians who desire, while living in the world, to live a more perfect life according to the spirit of the Benedictine Order.

2. Application requirements: The applicant must be twenty years of age, must have led a blameless life, and show love for St. Benedict and his Order.

3. Investiture: Three months after application the applicant receives the black scapular either from the abbot or his delegate; this investiture should occur in all seriousness and in a solemn manner.

4. Oblation: The act of oblation by which the applicant (now a novice) offers himself to the cloister, is made one year after investiture and resembles the regular profession. It is made in writing, is signed at the altar and is preserved in the archieves. With this oblation a candle is also offered to signify that the oblate furthermore wishes to offer some of his temporal possessions.

5. Conversion of morals: A summarized Rule of life was also drawn up at the Chapter.

[18] *Ibidem,* p 252; Heigl, "Die Weltlichen Oblaten des heiligen Benedictus", *Studien und Mittheilungen aus dem Bened. Orden,* II, p 359.

6. Pious works, such as the reception of monthly communion, certain prayers on fixed days, and the special veneration of Benedictine saints are to be cultivated.[16]

On January 17, 1871, the Congregation of Bishops and Regulars approved a new Rule for the Oblates, which was subsequently approved by the Sacred Congregation of Rites, June 4, 1888.[17] The Indulgences which were granted from 1888 to 1896 to the Oblates of Monte Cassino[18] were increased in 1898 and extended to all Secular Oblates of St. Benedict. Finally, July 23, 1904, Pius X approved anew the statutes, indulgences and privileges of the institute.[19]

The Congregation of Indulgences has declared that the present status of the Secular Oblates is practically the same as that of secular Tertiaries.[20]

[16]Heigl, *o. c.*, p 359-362.

[17]*A. S. S.*, XXVII, 440; Tachy, *Les Tiers Ordres*, p 12; Beringer, *Die Ablässe*, II, n. 409.

[18]E. g., by the S. C. of Indulgences Apr. 27, 1895 (*M. E.*, 9, Ser. I, vol. IX, 199 f).

[19]Beringer, *Die Ablässe*, II, n. 409; *Manual for Secular Oblates of St. Benedict*, p 24 f.

[20]Jan. 15, 1895 ad I (*A. S. S.*, XXVII, 440 f).

CHAPTER II

The Premonstratensian Movement

Almost from the very beginning the Order of Premontre founded by St. Norbert in 1121 consisted of the following classes: (a) priests and clerics under an Abbot or provost, known as the Canons Regular; (b) nuns who embraced the Rule of life as laid down by St. Norbert; (c) people who lived in the world, wore the white habit under their clothing and conformed their lives to the spirit of the Order.[1]

History relates that in 1128 Count Theobald came to Norbert with the purpose of giving his riches to the monastery and becoming a monk; but Norbert felt that he could accomplish more good in the world by being merely *affiliated* with the first Order, and he therefore invested Theobald with a white scapular as a symbol of the bond which united him to the Norbertine Order.[2] The institute thus founded was termed 'Fratres et Sorores ad Succurrendum'; it seems that this institution did not have the name of a Third Order until the foundation of the Third Orders by St. Francis and Dominic.[3]

[1]Kirkfleet, *History of St. Norbert,* p 106; Heimbucher, *Die Orden und Kongregationen der Katholischen Kirche,* II, p 58.

[2]Kirkfleet, *o. c.,* Le Paige, *Bibliotheca Praem. O.,* I, 311; Heimbucher, *l. c.*

[3]According to Le Paige, *l. c.,* Norbert gave them 'regulas quasdam'; cf. also *ASs.,* June, I, pp 920-923; Van Den Borne, *Die Anfänge des Franziskanischen Dritten Ordens (Franziskanische Studien,* Beiheft VIII) p 49 f.

Following the example of Theobald, many nobles as well as common people became affiliated with the Order of Premontre. The early Rules of the society which thus developed are the following: After postulants had received the scapular or white habit from the hands of the Abbot, their names were registered by the sacristan in the book of the fraternity. From this time onward, their obligations consisted in the daily recitation of a number of *Paters* and *Aves* in place of the canonical hours of the monks; they confessed and communicated at least seven times a year on the principal feasts. In addition to the fasts appointed by the Church, they were to fast on every Friday of the year, and to abstain during the time of Advent. These Rules did not bind under sin: the members merely bound themselves to the acceptance of the penance imposed at the discretion of the confessor.[4]

In the year 1135 a Contract of Brotherhood was made between the Canons of Notre Dame and the Canons of Premontre of St. Michael's Abbey in Antwerp, in which there was an agreement that the members of the Notre Dame par-

[4]Le Paige, *o. c.*, 312; it is doubtful however whether these Rules can be said to have originated at the time of Norbert; this is especially the case regarding the reception of the Sacraments. The monks themselves received communion only about seven times yearly, and for those who lived in outlying districts, the number was even less. Le Paige, *l. c.*, although attempting to prove the existence of these Rules at the time of Norbert, nevertheless in speaking of the members of the society using these Rules, says 'olim obligantur', as though the exact time at the most were indeterminate. The movement of the laity toward affiliation with the Order of Premontre at the time of Norbert is not denied, but in view of these difficulties, it is doubtful whether this movement could be resolved into what is now known as a Third Order. It would therefore seem that these Rules, especially those regarding the frequent reception of the Sacraments, had their origin at a later date when this frequent reception of the Sacraments (it was considered such in the twelfth century) was more in accord with the custom and trend of the times. Cf. Van Den Borne, *o. c.*, p 49-53.

ish who desire aggregation with the Premonstratensians may, after accepting the Rule of the Order, receive the Sacraments from them and be buried by them in their Churches.[5]

It seems that about the middle of the sixteenth century the custom of wearing the white scapular was somewhat modified, and that instead of this scapular, the members wore a medal of lead having on one side the figure of a host in a monstrance; this medal was suspended from the neck.[6] At the close of the seventeenth century, the 'Confraternity of the White Scapular' established in the Abbey of Beauport in Catholic Brittany received papal approbation.[7]

On May 22, 1751, Benedict XIV approved a Rule for the Third Order Secular of St. Norbert and granted many privileges to its members;[8] a new list of Indulgences was approved March 4, 1904.[9]

[5] The Bollandists (*ASs*, June, I, p 920-923) demonstrate that this had evident reference to what is now known as the Third Order Secular of St. Norbert.

[6] *Ibidem.*

[7] Hugo, *Annales O. Praem.*, I, 314.

[8] Auvrey, *Manuel du Tiers Ordre de Premontre*, p 32; Tachy, *Les Tiers Ordres;* p 15; Heimbucher, l. c. gives 1752 as the date of approval; the complete Rule is given in Auvrey, *o. c.*, and in Geudens, *Manual of the Third Order of St. Norbert.*

[9] S. C. of Indulg. (*A. S. S.*, XXXVI, 634-637).

CHAPTER III

The Humiliates

The development of the religious life in both clergy and laity received a new impetus in the twelfth century at the hands of the Humiliates. Their origin has commonly been connected with a group of Lombardian nobles whom the Emperor Henry II exiled to Germany in the year 1017. These noblemen were supposed to have been returned to their native land by command of the Emperor, on condition that they would form a sort of religious brotherhood, and cause no more political troubles.[1] The chronicle continues that these companies of both men and women persisted for more than a century without any recognized Rule, 'and they were called brethren of the Third Order'. Later St. Bernard (1134) is said to have given them permission to separate from their wives, and also to have given them a Rule.[2]

Zanoni rejects this old opinion and proves conclusively that the Humiliates do not go back farther than the second

[1]This chronicle is given in Tiraboschi, *Vetera Humiliatorum Monumenta*, III whose work is not accessible; the excerpt is taken from Davison, *Some forerunners of St. Francis of Assisi*, p 57; Brück, *Lehrbuch der Kirchengeschichte*, p 492, evidently bases the part of the Emperor Henry II on the same evidence.

[2]Davison, *l. c.*, Hergenrother-Hanlen, *Welzer und Welte's Kirchenlexikon*, VI, p 419 f; cf. also Hergenrother, *Theologische Bibliothek*, II, p 638.

half of the twelfth century.[3]

The part often attributed to St. John of Mede in the foundation of this organization[4] is also proved to be without foundation.

The impulses which produced this society seem to have been the fervent religious preaching and agitation especially among the lower classes; they fasted severely, did manual labor, and established communities of men and women engaged principally in the weaving of wool.[5] The anonymous Chronist of Laon speaks of certain citizens of Lombardy (1178) who lived a religious life in their homes, abstained from oaths and lawsuits, and took the name 'Humiliates' because of their poor clothing. Having requested the Pope to sanction their tenets, they were told that they might continue their mode of life provided they did this in humility and abstained from holding conventicles and preaching; they however defied the Apostolic command and incurred excommunication.[6]

Toward the end of the twelfth century the name 'Humiliate' had a heretical meaning among the people.[7]

The Chronist Buchard of Augsberg speaks of them being heretical *from the very beginning.*[8] The most plausible explanation, however, is that due to the letter of Innocent III to the bishop of Verona (1197)[9], an investigation was made

[3]Synopsis of Zanoni's arguments in Van Den Borne, *Die Anfänge des Franziskanischen Dritten Ordens (Franziskanische Studien,* Beiheft VIII), p 65 f, and in *A. F. H.*, VI [1913], p 172-175.

[4]Cf. Holweck, *A Biographical Dictionary of the Saints,* p 545; *ASs.,* Sept., VII, p 320-336.

[5]*A. F. H.,* VI [1913], p 173.

[6]*M. G. H. Ss.,* XXVI, p 449 f.

[7]Already in 1184 the name is mentioned in connection with an excommunication of those 'qui se Humiliatos vel Pauperes de Lugduno falso nomine mentiuntur.' (Mansi, Collectio Concilii, XXII, p 477).

[8]*M. G. H. Ss.,* XXIII, p 377.

[9]Migne, *P. L.,* CCXIV, 788 f.

which distinguished the true from the false, the former being reconciled to the Church and given a Rule by Innocent III June 7, 1201.[10] In the Bull of confirmation Innocent III reminded them of their former heretical tendencies; he approved three branches: the first, second, and third Orders. The latter was composed of men and women who lived at home with their families. According to Pierron, the Rule for the Third Order contained the following points:[11]

The greatest importance is laid upon the practice of humility, penance, obedience toward the prelates of the Church, patience and the suffering of injuries, prayer and the practice of mutual Christian charity.

Obligations: Whatever remained of the income resulting from their manual labor was to be distributed among the poor; tithes were paid to the clergy.

Wednesdays and Fridays were days of fasting with the following exceptions: Pentecost, the time from Christmas to Epiphany, and the Holy Days of the Church.

The time of the canonical hours was observed by the recitation of Seven *Our Fathers,* in addition to the recitation of the *Apostles' Creed* at Compline and Prime.

They were especially admonished to dress plainly, to fulfill their conjugal obligations faithfully, and to assist one another in time of sickness.

All were obliged to attend the funerals of deceased brethren, and recite prescribed prayers for the repose of their souls.

They were to live at peace with their fellow men, and to

[10] *A. F. H.*, VI [1913], p 173; Davison, *Some Forerunners of St. Francis of Assisi,* p 59 f; Van Den Borne, *Die Anfänge des Franzis-Kanischen Dritten Ordens (Franziskanische Studien,* Beiheft VIII) p 66; Buchberger, *Kirchliches Handlexikon,* I, p 2046, is of the opinion that the Humiliates lapsed into the heresy of the Waldenses and were excommunicated toward the end of the twelfth century.

[11] Van Den Borne, *o. c.,* p 67 f.

repair all injury to their brethren. Daily prayers were required for the deceased, and for peace in the Church and among all Christian peoples. Prayer was required at all meals, as well as moderation in eating and drinking.

Permission was given to assemble every Sunday in a fitting place, where one of the brethren versed in religion was to give an instruction after having obtained the permission of the diocesan bishop. They were forbidden to preach about faith or the Sacraments.[12]

A comparison of these Rules with those of the primitive Franciscan Tertiaries shows a striking resemblance, and in many instances an identical application. Especially is this noticeable regarding the obligation of fealty to the Church, the restoration of ill-gotten goods, prayers for the dead, attendance at funerals, and the alleviation of the sufferings of the sick and the poor. Their refusal to take an oath had the same effect as in the Franciscan Third Order: the breaking down of the feudal system, and the consequent collision of the Humiliates with the civil authorities, with whom Innocent III remonstrated in their behalf.[13]

This short sketch is sufficient to indicate the great influence which the Rule of the Humiliates exercised upon the regulations drawn up for the Franciscan Tertiaries by St. Francis and Cardinal Ugolino.[14]

The Humiliates gradually broke up in the beginning of the sixteenth century, so that the Order is now no longer in existence.[15]

[12]This seems to be a warning not to relapse into their former heretical sermons.

[13]Cuthbert, *Life of St. Francis of Assisi,* p 336; Felder, *The Ideals of St. Francis of Assisi,* p 292 f.

[14]Cf. the first Rule of the Third Order of St. Francis in the appendix to this treatise; *A. F. H.,* VI [1913], p 174.

[15]*Ibidem;* Davison, *Some Forerunners of St. Francis of Assisi,* p 68 f.

CHAPTER IV

The Dominican Third Order Secular

There is a variance of opinion regarding the exact foundation of the Third Order Secular of St. Dominic. According to the *Annales* of the Dominican Order, this institution at its inception had both a religious and military aspect; the male members were to combat the heresies condemned by the Church and, if necessary, to defend the possessions of the Church with physical force, while their wives and relatives were to live lives of piety and prayer.[1]

A second opinion would have it that it was originally an order of penance similar to the Franciscan Third Order Secular; this was under the care of the Friars Preachers whose influence over them became more pronounced as time progressed; later a society previously organized for combating heresies (known as the Militia of Jesus Christ) lost its military aspect and became a part of the Third Order.[2]

The opinion of Blessed Raymond of Capua seems to possess the greatest probability. According to him the Third Order of St. Dominic arose from the Militia of Jesus Christ.[3] The men were required under oath to fulfill this office; their wives and relatives were also obliged under oath not to hinder the men in the fulfillment of this duty; Dominic him-

[1] *Annales O. Praed.*, I, p 232 f.

[2] Jarret, "The Third Order of St. Dominic", *Catholic Encyclopedia,* XIV, p .638.

[3] The commission to organize this association seems to have been given to St. Dominic by the bishop of Tolouse-Heimbucher, *o. c.*, II, p 169.

self called these the Militia of Jesus Christ. When these military duties were no longer necessary, the Holy See changed their name to 'Fratres de Poenitentia S. Dominici'.[5]

December 22, 1227, Gregory IX approved and confirmed their object of defending the faith.[6]

The opinion of Blessed Raymond of Capua is implicitly denied by Malvenda when he places the Bull, *Detestanda humani generis,* of Gregory IX (1227 or 1228) in the Dominican Bullarium[7]; he thus claims that this Bull has reference to the Dominican Tertiaries. But this seems to be false, for historians (Raymond of Capua, S. Antoninus, and an anonymous Dominican historian) agree that the name *Fratres de Poenitentia* was not applied to the Dominican lay society until after the death of Dominic, which occurred in 1234. How, then, can this Bull of 1227 which is given in favor of the *Fratres de Poenitentia,* have reference to those of the Dominicans at a time when they were not known by such a name? It follows, therefore, that this Bull has evident reference to the 'Fratres de Poenitentia *S. Francisci*'.[8] Sbaralea also demonstrates that this Bull was placed in the Bullarium of the Dominican Order by mistake.[9]

However the Constitution *Ut cum majori* of November 21, 1234, seems to have reference to the Fratres de Poenitentia

[5] *ASs.*, Aug., I, p 419; in effect the same opinion is held by: Tachy, *Les Tiers Ordres,* p 13; Heimbucher, *o. c.,* p 169 f; Hergenrother, *Theologische Bibliothek,* II, p 629 f; Currier, *History of Religious Orders,* p 280; Chelodi, *Jus de Personis,* n. 302; Vermeersch-Creusen, *Epitome,* n. 788; Prümmer, *Manuale Juris Canonici,* Q. 270; Drane, *The History of St. Dominic,* p 243-245; cf. also [ ], *The English Dominican Province,* p 303 f; for the Rule of the Militia, cf. Frederici, *Historia de Cavalieri Gaudenti,* II, p 12 f.

[6] Bull, *Egrediens Hereticorum* (*Bull. O. Praed.,* I, n. 19, p 25).

[7] *Bull. O. Praed.,* I, n. 25, p 27 f.

[8] *ASs.,* Aug., I, p 420 f; cf. Drane, *The History of St. Dominic,* p 245.

[9] *Bull. Franc.,* I, n. 20, p 40.

S. Dominici as well as those of the Franciscans, for at this time both Franciscan and Dominican Tertiaries were known as 'Poenitents'.[11]

In the beginning the Dominican Tertiaries had no definite Rules, so that in 1285 the Minister-General of the Friars Preachers, Munon di Zamora, drew up definite Regulations,[12] which were approved by Innocent VII in 1405 and by Eugene IV in 1439.[13]

[11]Cf. *ASs.*, l. c.; *Annales O. Praed.*, I, p 236 f.

[12]Mortier, *Histoire des Maitres Généreaux de L'Ordre des Frères Prêcheurs,* II, p 221 f.

[13]Buchberger, *Kirchlickes Handlexikon,* II, p 2326; for a list of recent indulgences and privileges granted to the Order cf. *A. S. S.*, XXXIX, 553-558.

CHAPTER V

The Third Order Secular of St. Francis

Article I
Foundation and First Rule

The preceding chapters have attempted to give an idea of the tendency on the part of the laity to connect themselves in some manner with the religious life, while still living in the world. It is but natural that this should have exercised great influence on the origin and development of the Franciscan Third Order.[1]

In the time of St. Francis the tendency of the people in this regard is first brought to light by the great influence he and his disciples exercised by their preaching; many were thus attracted by the man of God.[2]

That this preaching bore great fruit is attested by the 'Legend of the Three Companions', which relates that the people led a more mortified life in their homes.[3]

[1]This is admitted by historians and canonists: cf. above chapter I.

[2]"* * * veritatem fidentissime loquebantur, ita ut etiam litteratissimi viri, gloria et dignitate pollentes, ejus mirarentur sermones et timore utili ejus presentia terrerentur. Currebant viri, currebant et feminae, festinabant cleri (ci), accelerabant religiosi, ut viderent et audirent sanctum Dei, qui homo alterius saeculi videbatur. Omnis aetas, omnisque sexus properabat cernere mirabilia, quae noviter Dominus per servum suum operabatur in mundo * * *"—Legenda Prima, XV (*S. Francisci Vita et Miracula*, ed. Alenconiensis, p 38 f).

[3]*ASs.*, October, II, p 737.

The first definite thought and purpose in the mind of Francis to connect all classes of people in some manner with the First Order seems to be contained in his letter 'to all Christians, religious, clerics and laity, men and women, to all who dwell in the whole world,"[4] in which he exhorts them to lead a more christian life, as he sets forth in the letter. "In practice it [the letter] would be interpreted by those living in the world to demand a closer or more distant approximation to the observance of the brethren themselves. . . . But the letter was to them in very fact, a rule of life to which they sought to conform their conduct. . . . They did not at first nor for some years constitute a separate organization from the brethren themselves: in the larger sense they were considered members of the fraternity, even as Clare and her sisters were."[5]

According to Thomas of Celano, the first definite idea of a Third Order arose in the mind of Francis when he performed a miracle while preaching at Alviano.[6] On account of this miracle and the great eloquence of Francis, the multitude wished to become his disciples. Realizing this to be incompatible with their state of life in the world, the Saint nevertheless promised that he would provide for them; whereupon he considered establishing a Third Order 'qui

[4]The letter may be found in, Robinson, *The writings of St. Francis,* p 98-108 (he places the date of the letter at 1215-p 96); [ ], *Works of St. Francis of Assisi,* p 1-9; Boehmer, *Analekten zur Geschichte des Franzikus von Assisi,* p 49-57; Little, *Francis of Assisi,* p 164 also prefers the date as 1215; Wadding, *Annales Minorum,* ad an. 1213, places the date of the letter to this year.

[5]Cuthbert, *Life of St. Francis,* p 331.

[6]Legenda Prima, XXI, 59 (*S. Francisci Vita et Miracula,* ed. Alenconiensis, p 62); in *Actus B. Francisci,* by Sabatier, p 57, this incident is laid in Cannara; Wadding, *o. c.* ad an. 1212, n. 32, gives the name of the town as Alviano; in *Fioretti,* cap. 16, the name is mentioned as Savurniano.

dicitur continentium'.[7]

The influence caused by the letter and the latter incident, coupled with the agitation already in the minds of the faithful caused by the religious forerunners of St. Francis, seem to have been the direct impelling motive for the establishment of a Third Order Secular by the Saint.

The opinion that the Third Order separated from the First and was thus developed[8] has been severely criticized.[9]

The real foundation of the Third Order seems to have occurred during the year 1221[10] at Fienza and the surrounding

[7]Jorgensen, *St. Francis of Assisi*, p 240 f.

[8]Mandonnet, *Les Origines de L'Ordo de Poenitentia (Compte Rendu du IV Congres Scientifique International des Catholiques)*, p 183-215.

[9]Little, *A Guide to Franciscan Studies*, p 60; *A. F. H.*, XIII [1920], p 76-" * * * "S. Franciscus tres ordines instituit, tribuens unicuique normam vitae"; Bernard of Besse, "Liber de Laudibus", *Analecta Franciscana*, III, p 679-"Doctrinae Francisci elucet maxime fructus in tribus ab eo statutis ordinibus"; "I cannot accept unreservedly the conclusions of M. Sabatier and P. Mandonnet O. P. that in the beginning of the Franciscan fraternity these informal disciples [those who lived in the world according to the Franciscan spirit, being fired by the influence of Francis] who afterward became the nucleus of the Third Order, were considered members of the fraternity in the same sense as the friars and the sisters of San Damiano * * * There is no evidence that people professing this Rule separated, one group forming the First Order and another the Third". (Cuthbert, *o. c.*, p 323; Bihl (*A. F. H.*, VI [1913], p 175 in speaking of the historian Zanoni, makes the following remark: "Ipse Z. [Zanoni] *Male* sequitur hypotheses P. Mandonnet * * *"; cf. Wyngaert, "Examen des Theories du R. P. Mandonnet sur L'Ordo de Poenitentia", *Neerlandia Franciscana*, VI; Van Den Borne, *Die Anfänge des Franziskanischen Dritten Ordens, o. c.*, p 92.

[10]*Bull. Franc.*, I, n. 8; in speaking of the Bull, *Significatum est nobis*, which was given to the Penitents [Tertiaries] at this time by Honorius III, Sbaralea, the author of the *Bullarium Franciscanum*, makes the following comment: "Nimirum fratres tertii ordinis dicti de poenitentia hoc anno mense Junio a S. P. Francisco institutum primum apud Canaria oppidum prope Assisium, exinde apud alia loca et civitates ut perhibet laudibilis Waddingus"; Wadding, *Annales Minorum*, ad an. 1221, n. 12 mentions the same town; Marianus,

country.[11] Cardinal Hugolino and St. Francis collaborated in drawing up the Rule.[12] There is also the express testimony of Bernard of Besse that Francis founded a Third Order.[13] The reason that this institution is called a *Third* Order is because of its chronological foundation after the *First* Order (Regulars) and *Second* Order (Poor Clares) respectively.

However all indications point to the fact that even before the explicit establishment of the Rule by the Saint and Cardinal Hugolino, many of the faithful had already received special norms of life from the hands of Francis;[14] the

"Compendium Chronicorum FF. Minorum", *A. F. H.*, II [1909], p 96, mentions the year as being 1220—"Anno Domini 1220 beatus Franciscus applicuit Venetias et Bononiam, ubi ab omnibus honorifice receptus fuit cum gaudium et omnium applausu, et praecipue a Domino Hugolino, legato Sanctae Romanae Ecclesiae, cum Florentiam veniens, et reperiens devotionem maximam populi ad poentitentiam animati, composuit regulam pro viris et mulieribus a matrimonio ligatis". However, the date which Marianus gives seems to be false, for Hugolino was not in Florence at that time (1220)—cf. *A. F. H.*, II [1909], p 96, n. 10; Vermeersch, *Periodica*, (163).

[11] Van Den Borne, *Die Anfänge des Franziskanischen Dritten Ordens, o. c.*, p 127 mentions this town as possessing the greatest probability; cf, also Müller, *Die Anfänge des Minoritenordens*, p 133 f.

[12] Wyngaert, "De Tertio Ordine S. Francisci", *A. F. H.*, XIII [1920], after a critical examination, draws the following conclusion: "Card. Hugolinus anno 1221, legatione fungens et inveniens quosdam fratres de poenitentia composuit regulam". Benedict XV, const., *Sacra Propediem*, Jan. 6, 1921 (*A. A. S.*, XIII [1921], 35) also states that Cardinal Hugolino assisted Francis in drawing up the Rules.

[13] "Liber de Laudibus", *Analecta Franciscana*, III, p 679—"Doctrinae Francisci elucet maxime fructus in tribus ab eo statutis ordinibus". p 686—"Tertius est Ordo fratrum et sororum de poenitentia, clericis, laicis, virginibus et conjugatis communis, cujus propositum est in domibus propriis honeste vivere * * *".

[14] Jorgensen, *St. Francis of Assisi*, p. 242; Van Den Wyngaert, "De Sanctis et Beatis Tertii Ordinis", *A. F. H.*, XIV [1921], p. 3: "Nam priusquam regula quae nobis ut antiquior nota est, pro penientibus redacta est et eis a Cardinali Hugolino imposita fuit, S. Franciscus

letter which he wrote to all the faithful may be cited as a good example of these indications.

According to Wadding,[15] the first reception into the Third Order took place at Gagniani, not far from 'Podii Bonantis, alias Bonitii', when Francis garbed Luchesius with the first habit of the penitential Order. The first Rule written by the Saint and Cardinal Hugolino was discovered by Sabatier about twenty years ago in the Franciscan Monastery of Capistrano in the Abruzzi;[16] he edited it in his *Regula Antiqua Fratrum et Sororum de Poenitentia.*[17]

The first five chapters and the first three numbers of the sixth chapter date from the year 1221; the remaining six chapters show some retouching from 1221 to 1228 or 1229. The last (thirteenth) seems to have been gradually added up to the year 1247. Despite these additions the Rule retains the same tenor throughout.[18]

The arrangement of the matter in the Rule is also rather faulty; thus the fourth chapter is separated from the fifth although both treat of prayer, while other chapters, e. g.

quamdam normam vitae cujus indolem ignoramus, eisdem tribuerat". Cf. Cuthbert, *Life of St. Francis,* p. 323 f; Van Den Borne, *Die Anfänge des Franziskanischen Dritten Ordens, o. c.,* p. 124 f.

[15] Wadding, *Annales Minorum,* ad an. 1221, n. 13; cf. also *ASs.,* April, III, pp. 605 f; *Officia Propria O. F. M. Conv.,* p. 141; Vermeersch, *Periodica,* XIII, (163).

[16] Callaey, *The Third Order of St. Francis,* p. 13.

[17] *Opuscules de Critique Historique,* I, pp. 16-30; another version of the Rule was edited by Lemmens, "Regula Antiqua Ordinis de Poenitentia (1221) juxta Novum Codicem", *A. F. H.,* VI [1913], p. 242-250; Oliger edited a Rule of 1289 part of which goes to the original Rule of 1221: "Expositio Brevis Regulae Antiquae III Ordinis S. Francisci", *A. F. H.,* XIV [1921], p. 122-129; the original Rule discovered by Sabatier is often called the *Capistran Rule* on account of the place where it was found.

[18] To substantiate these assertions the reader is referred to the *Regula Antiqua* as edited by Sabatier; it is reprinted in extenso in the appendix below pp. 177-185; the disposition and the repetition of the identical

VIII, X and XIII, contain more matter than is indicated in their title.

The Rule contains the following points:

The first chapter demands that the Tertiaries be garbed in simple dress, and that they do not take part in, or contribute toward frivolous amusements; the visitor is empowered to interpret the Rule regarding dress.

Only two meals should be eaten a day except by the sick; they should abstain from meat on all days excepting Sunday, Tuesday, Thursday and certain feasts; again they are excused on account of sickness and traveling; besides observing the ordinary ecclesiastical fasts, they are to fast on Wednesdays and Fridays from the feast of All Saints to Easter; a continual fast is to be observed from the feast of St. Martin to Christmas, and from Quinquagesima Sunday till Easter, unless legitimately dispensed on account of sickness or other necessity (II-III).

Clerics shall recite the canonical hours of the Church; the laity, psalms and other prescribed prayers in their stead; the sick are excused from this recitation. Unless legitimately prevented, all should attend matins during the Lent of St. Martin and also during the Great Lent. Confession and Communion is prescribed three times yearly (IV-VI, 1).

Past debts must be satisfied; the brethren should always speak with decorum and abstain from taking oaths except in those contingencies which are allowed by the Roman

matter with slight changes clearly indicate gradual additions and changes; for complete arguments cf. Mandonnet, *Les Regles et Le Gouvernement de L'Ordo de Poenitentia au XIII Siècle* (*Opuscules de Critique Historique*, I, p. 143-250); Wyngaert, "De Tertio Ordine S. Francisci", *A. F. H.*, XIII [1920], p. 3-67; Bughetti, "Prima Regula Tertii Ordinis", *A. F. H.*, XIV [1921], p. 109-121; proof of these changes and additions will be given from time to time throughout this dissertation.

Pontiff. Deadly weapons cannot be carried (the remainder of VI).

All are required to attend Mass in a body monthly, where a religious discourse shall be given by a religious; at this service dues must be paid to the treasurer for assisting the sick and the poor, as well as for funeral expenses. The poor and the sick shall be visited weekly by the ministers or their delegate, who are to render them assistance from the common fund. Tertiaries are to attend the funerals of the brethren and recite prayers for them within the octave of their death. Clerics shall say three Masses yearly for the dead; the laity shall recite prayers (VII-IX).

Those who have not satisfied all their obligations and made peace with their enemies cannot become members; heretics are also excluded. After a year's probation a novice is received into the Order by promising to obey the Rules of the organization, whereupon his name is written in the register. Within three months of profession, members are to draw up their will. Those who are incorrigible are to be expelled from the society by the visitor, after having obtained the advice of the more prudent brethren (X, 1, 5-10; XI; XII, 1-2).

Authority in the Third Order:

(a) The diocesan bishop is to intervene in the event of conflict between the rights of the Tertiaries and civil authority (X, 2-3). Those suspected of heresy must be cleared of this charge by him before entering the Order. Hence his permission was not ordinarily required for reception.

(b) The visitor possesses great authority in the Order: the quality of clothing and ornaments is subject to his judgment (I, 6); transgressors of the Rule must repair any scandal according to his discretion (X, 9); transgressions of the Rule must be reported to him (XII, 1), and it is he who, after having been informed of the obstinacy of an incorrigible Tertiary by the ministers, pronounces expulsion after a consultation with the more prudent brethren (XII, 2). Scandals must also be reported to him (XII, 4). The visitor may dispense from every point of the Rule in cases where he deems fit (XII, 5).

(c) The ministers seem to be considered as the local superiors of the society. They are elected yearly by the retiring ministers and their counselors (XII, 6); no one should refuse to accept an office for which he has been designated. The ministers receive applicants into the novitiate after due investigation; it is their duty to instruct novices in the Rule (X, 5), and they may also receive into the Order upon the advice of judicious Tertiaries; they may dispense from the ordinary mode of reception (X, 7-11). They are to keep vigil concerning discordances among the brethren (X, 2). Monthly meetings should be called by them at which, according to their discretion, money should be collected for the sick and poor (VII, 1-2), who are to be cared for through the ministers (VIII, 1).

(d) A minor official known as the treasurer is the administrator of the funds and distributes the alms collected at the monthly meetings (VII, 2; XII, 6).

Chapter thirteen was added at a considerably later date as the contents indicate: e. g. VI, 1 prescribes confession and communion three times yearly, while XIII, 5 states that the Tertiaries shall confess monthly; again XIII, 6 is a repetition of VII, 1, with slight changes. The addition of XIII, 2; 4-5 will be treated in the next article. Other insertions in the Rule which came about through papal decrees will also be treated as the occasion demands.

Article II

The Government of the Third Order Secular of St Francis

Relations with the Friars Minor

I Period: From its Foundation till the Time of Pope Benedict XIII

The summary of the primitive Rules given in the previous article clearly indicate that the entire government of the Third Order rested *ipso jure* with the Tertiaries themselves, from whom their officials were chosen. The ordinary of the place is accorded no authority beyond that of interceding in their behalf with the secular powers in case of conflict (X, 2-3) and in deciding the suspicion of heresy in reference to postulants (X, 1). In stating that the entire government was vested in the Tertiaries, it is not intended to imply that the Friars Minor had nothing to do with the direction of the Third Order. The very fact that St. Francis had founded the society would logically postulate some connection with the First Order. But to assert on the other hand, that the Friars Minor had rights (*jura*) founded in law toward the Tertiaries is going beyond the contents of the Rule as well as papal documents now available.

Fr. Callaey is of the belief that at the monthly meetings, the preacher mentioned in the Rule as 'unum religiosum'[1] may have been a Friar Minor: "The expression 'Unum religiosum' seems to have had a very broad meaning and to imply that the Tertiaries were free to choose their preachers from among the secular clergy or even a layman; but it is equally probable that the expression indicates no one else but a Friar Minor".[2]

[1] VII, 3.

[2] Callaey, *The Third Order of St. Francis*, p. 95, n. 13.

Regarding the power of the visitor and the ministers, this seems to have changed at times. Sabatier describes the authority of the visitor of the thirteenth century in the following sense: "Dans la langue du XIIIe siècle, le mot de *visitator* désigne d'ordinaire des inspecteurs chargés avant tout d'assurer le fonctionnement régulier de la discipline, ce sont les dignitaires de la police ecclésiastique".[3] Sometimes the visitor appears as a mere corrector;[4] at other times as having real legislative power which is over that of the ministers;[5] then again the authority of the ministers and the visitor seems to be equal.[6]

Visitation by the bishop was not introduced until the year 1234, when this authority was given to him by Gregory IX: *"Per apostolica vobis scripta mandamus, quatenus ud visitationem et correctionem eorum quilibet in sua dioecesi sollicite intendentes, et habentes ipsos ob reverentiam Sedis Apostolicae et Nostram propensius commendatos, nec molestiis, nec permittas eosdem, quantum in vobis fuerit, molestari indebite".*[7] From this it is to be inferred that these molestations to which the pontiff refers were to be stopped by the visitation and intercession of the bishops, and that they did not cease before because the bishops had performed this office up to this time; the Rule (i. e., up to chapter thirteen, which was added at a considerable later date) did not require a priest as visitor;[7*] hence it seems that up to the year 1234—when the ordinary of the place assumed this office—it was filled neither by a secular priest nor by a Friar Minor, but by a layman.

[3] *Opuscles de Critique Historique,* I, p. 19; the italics belong to the original author.

[4] I, 6; X, 9; XII, 1, 2, 4, 7.

[5] XII, 2.

[6] XIII, 1, 4, 6, 9, 14, 15.

[7] Bull, *Ut cum majori,* Nov. 21, 1234 (*Bull. Franc.,* I, n. 149, p. 142 f).

Although the Original Rule did not give the Friars Minor any part in the government of the Third Order, it seems that they took some part in the spiritual direction of the local fraternities, according to the testimony of Bernard of Besse: *"Tertius est Ordo fratrum et sororum de poenitentia . . . Istis a principio frater assignabatur minister";*[8] but even this contact which the Friars Minor maintained with the local organizations in the beginning gradually vanished, according to the same testimony, which continues: *"sed nunc suis in terra dimmituntur Ministris, ut tamen a fratribus tamquam confratres et codem patre geniti consiliis et auxiliis foveantur".*[9]

Beginning with chapter seven, ministers are mentioned, who again did not require any sacerdotal character. Using the testimony of Bernard of Besse, it seems that in the beginning the Friars Minor exercised this office, and that chapter seven was inserted in the Rule at a time when, according to Bernard of Besse, the direct contact with the local fraternities was no longer kept up by the latter; this change of the office of minister from the Friars Minor to two members of the Third Order occurred about 1227, according to Wyngaert,[10] and was inserted in the Rule at that time. There are no documents from which the duties of the minister mentioned by Bernard of Besse can be deduced. Despite the fact that this office seems to have been exercised by the Friars Minor, nowhere is there any proof that the Tertiaries were *subject* to them, nor that they had any rights

[7*] A priest is not mentioned as fulfilling this office, nor do his duties require a sacerdotal character; cf. Mandonnet, *Les Regles et le Gouvernement de L'Ordo de Poenitentia au XIII Siècle* (*Opuscules de Critique Historique,* I) p. 183 f; Sabatier, *Regula Antiqua Fratrum et Sororum de Poenitentia* (*Ibidem*), p. 12.

[8] "Liber de Laudibus", *Analecta Franciscana,* III, p. 686.

[9] *Ibidem.*

[10] *A. F. H.*, XIII [1920], p. 72.

(*jura*) toward the Third Order *which they could assert*, such as they received through later papal decrees.

Chapter thirteen, beginning with the fourth number up to the tenth, was inserted about 1247 when Innocent IV conceded the first papal jurisdiction to the Friars Minor over the Tertiaries of Italy. For the purposes of comparison, the dispositive part of the Bull, and the Rule itself, will be quoted: *"Nos eorum precibus annuentes discretioni vestrae praesertim auctoritate mandamus, quatenus ipsis opportunis temporibus, per vos, et Fratres vestri Ordinis ad hoc idoneos visitationis officium independentes, et instruentes regularibus disciplinis, corrigatis, reformetis eosdem, tam in capite, quam in membris, quae correctionis, et visitationis officio noveritis indigere"*.[11] Here the Friars Minor are clearly given the right of spiritual direction over the Third Order in Italy. Note is also to be taken of the word *'instruentes'*, from which it may also be concluded that they took over the office of instructor, which is mentioned in the original Rule as *'unum religiosum'*.[12] In the Rule[13] there is the following: " . . . *petant a ministro vel custode fratrum Minorum unum fratrem Minorem de conventu, cujus fratris consilio et voluntate fratrum ista fraternitas gubernetur in omnibus et regatur. Et quando ille frater* [*Minor*] *recederet de conventu, petant alium loco ejus, ita quod semper consilio fratrum Minorum regatur ista fraternitas quae a beato Francisco habuit fundamentum*". The similarity between the words of the Bull and the Rule indicates that the latter was formulated and placed in the regulations on account of the former. Another argument can be deduced from the words *'de conventu'*: this term was not in use before the middle of the

[11] Bull. *Vota devotorum,* June 13, 1247 (*Bull. Franc.*, I, n. 210, p. 464).

[12] VII, 3.

[13] XIII, 4-5.

thirteenth century,[14] therefore neither was it placed in the Rule before that time.

The Bull quoted was given in favor of the Friars Minor after the Tertiaries of Southern and Central Italy had petitioned Innocent IV to allow the Friars Minor to perform the office of visitation instead of the bishops; they feared that the bishops and pastors of Italy, many of whom had complained in a letter to the Emperor Frederic II that the two 'mendicant orders had lessened their [the bishops' and pastors'] popularity by establishing two new brotherhoods, and enrolling so many men and women that hardly one person can be found who is not a member.'[15]

Despite the fact that this jurisdiction over the Tertiaries was thus taken away from the bishops and given to the Friars Minor, Innocent IV allowed the bishops of Lombardy who were antagonistic to the cause of Frederic II to retain authority over the Tertiaries, especially regarding visitation.[16] The same pontiff excommunicated Frederic and decreed that all who would adhere to him would incur the same censure.[17] Many who later repented of their adherence to the Emperor turned toward the Franciscan Third Order as a refuge, whereupon Innocent granted faculties to the Friars Minor Provincials to absolve them for the purpose of entering the Order.[18]

[14] Holzapfel, *Manuale Historiae O. F. M.*, p. 71 f; cf. Wyngaert, "De Tertio Ordine S. Francisci", *A. F. H.*, XIII [1920], p. 73, note 3.

[15] Callaey, *The Third Order of St. Francis*, p. 33; the two brotherhoods referred to are of course the Third Orders Secular of St. Francis and Dominic; this letter has commonly been attributed to Peter de Vinea, a counselor of Frederic II; the authorship, however, is as given above—cf. Callaey, *o. c.*, p. 88-94; p. 97, note 9.

[16] Nov. 10, 1248 (*Bull. Franc. Epitome*, n. 518).

[17] Parsons, *Studies in Church History*, II, p. 375 f.

[18] "Cupientes animarum periculis obviare, absolvendi eos, qui Fratres de Poenitentia in Italia, et Regno Siciliae Ordinem intraverint, ab excommunicationis sententia, si quam fovendo F. R. quondam Imperatori,

At the same time this favor is evidence of the esteem in which the Third Order was held as a means of combating those who were false to their promises of adherence to the Church. There is no doubt that the large numbers of the laity who thus forsook their allegiance to Frederic greatly weakened his power.

Some say that between the years 1257-1274 (the Generalate of St. Bonaventure) the Friars Minor had very little to do with the Third Order Secular; as a proof they put forth the question which was said to have been included in a letter written to the Saint: *"Why do the Friars Minor not favor the Order of Penance"*? However, it is doubtful whether this letter,[19] which also contains the answer of the Saint, is authentic.[20] On the other hand there is evidence that the relations between the Friars Minor and the Tertiaries gradually became lessened, for in 1264 the Tertiaries of San Gemignano were permitted to receive the sacraments in times of interdict in the parish church, but *not* in the Church of the Friars Minor.[21] There are, however, individual instances of friendly relations between the two Orders.[22]

In 1289 Nicholas IV solemnly approved the Third Order

et fautoribus ejus, postquam excommunicatus extitit, incurrerunt; dummodo super eum quod foverunt, vel adhaererunt, de stando mandatis Ecclesiae, et de non favendo, ac adhaerendo eo de caetero praestent cautionem juratoriam, et aliam etiam congruentem; auctoritate vobis praesentium concedimus facultatem".—Bull, *Cupientes animarum*, Sept. 24, 1247 (*Bull. Franc.*, *I*, n. 241, p. 492 f).

[19] Cf. *A. F. H.*, II [1909], p. 67, n. 2; *S. Bonuventurae Opera Omnia*, VIII, p. 368 f.

[20] Cf. Wyngaert, "De Tertio Ordine S. Francisci", *A. F. H.*, XIII [1920], p. 74, n. 5.

[21] Urban IV, July 5, 1264 (*Bull. Franc. Epitome*, n. 1200).

[22] Cf. *o. c.*, *n.* 1304; *Bull. Franc.*, III, n. 161, p. 153; *A. F. H.*, I [1908], p. 549, X, where the Statutes of the Tertiaries of Brescia mention that a Friar Minor should be summoned in case of discordance among the brethren.

and issued a new Rule. The part relating to the Friars Minor bears out the assertion that their relations with the Tertiaries had gradually become weaker, for the pontiff only *advises* that the reformers and visitors should be taken from the Friars Minor, who are to be designated by their guardian; lay persons are forbidden to exercise the office of visitation.[23]

But even this mild measure of subjection to the Friars Minor was opposed by many of the Tertiaries who openly rebelled against it; the pontiff responded to the rebillious Tertiaries by cutting them off from all privileges, past or future, granted to Tertiaries by the Apostolic See. To those who were not opposed to this Rule, he granted permission to establish fraternities separate from the disobedient Tertiaries and to elect their own ministers.[24] The bishop of Florence, becoming vexed because the Tertiaries of that place had followed the advice of the pontiff in regard to the visitors, seized their official documents and prohibited them from administering the goods which they had collected for the benefit of the poor. Under threat of more severe measures, the bishop of Florence was commanded to restore all properties to the Tertiaries.[25]

[23] "Quia vero praesens vivendi foram institutionem a beato Francisco praelibato suscepit, *consulimus*, ut visitatores et informatores de Fratrum Minorum Ordine assumantur, quos custodes vel guardiani ejusdem Ordinis cum super hoc requisiti fuerint, duxerint assignandos. Nolumus tamen congregationem hujusmodi a laico visitari". (Chap. XVI of the Rule contained in this Bull).—Bull, *Supra montem*, Aug. 17, 1289 (*Bull. Franc.*, IV, n. 150, p. 94); however the compiler of the *Bullarium* places the date as the 18th. In the *Bull. Franc. Epitome*, p. 302, the 19th is mentioned; Wadding, *Annales Minorum*, ad an. 1221, places the date for that year—this is obviously incorrect (cf. *A. F. H.*, XIII [1920], p. 77); the *Fontes*, n. 588 refer to this constitution as having been issued on the 19th.

[24] Bull, *Unigenitus Dei Filius*, Aug. 8, 1290 (*Bull. Franc. Epitome*, n. 52, p. 305 f).

[25] Bull, *Ad audiendam*, Sept. 20, 1291 (*o. c.*, n. 1968, p. 198).

Many of the Tertiaries fell into the errors of the Beguines and the Beghards concerning the state of perfection, and were excommunicated by Clement V;[26] but in spite of this, the same pontiff approved of the Rule of the Third Order.[27] John XXII also praised the Third Order and its spiritual guides, the Friars Minor.[28]

Eugene IV reaffirmed the jurisdiction over the Tertiaries as accorded by Nicholas IV to the Friars Minor,[29] and in several instances and places subjected the Tertiaries to the jurisdiction of the Franciscans.[30] Other pontiffs did the same.[31]

After the division of the First Order into the Friars Minor Conventual and Friars Minor Observant, Pope Sixtus IV gave the Minister-General of the Friars Minor (Conventual) as well as the Vicar-General of the Observants complete authority over the Tertiaries: to garb with the habit, receive into the Order, to perform the canonical visitation, to reform them both in head and members, and to appoint a priest of the First Order as confessor. This authority was to be the same as that granted by Innocent IV to the Franciscan Superiors over the Tertiaries of Italy,[32] with the additional privilege of receiving into the Order and appointing a con-

[26] Cf. Denziger-Bannwart, *Enchyridion Symbolorum*, nn. 471-478; Van Den Borne, "Analecta de Tertio Ordine", *A. F. H.*, IX [1916], p. 127 f.

[27] Bull, *Tenorem cujusdam*, Aug. 30, 1308 (*Orbis Seraphicus*, II, 789).

[28] *Orbis Seraphicus*, II, 793 f; cf. Oliger, "Documenta Inedita ad Hist. Fraticel. Spectantia", *A. F. H.*, VI [1913], p. 728.

[29] Nov. 15, 1431 (*Orbis Seraphicus*, II, 890 f).

[30] Bull, *Exposcit*, Apr. 28, 1444 (*o. c.*, B02-804); cf. Flaminio di Parma, *Memorie instoriche delle chiese e conventi dell' Osservante e Reformati Prov. di Bologna*, I, p. 428.

[31] Flaminio di Parma, *o. c.*, p. 430; Alexander VII (Orbis Seraphicus, II, 804 f); Pius II, Bull, *Pia Deo*, July 13, 1462 (*o. c.*, 893).

[32] Cf. above note 11.

fessor.[83]

The most important points of this concession are: (a) the office of visitation which heretofore had pertained to the ordinary of the place (it was only a counsel or wish of Nicholas IV that the Friars Minor be the visitors, hence they had not the canonical right) was now transferred for all times to the Superiors of the Franciscan Order; (b) this seems to be the first instance where the Friars Minor are empowered by papal authority to receive into the Third Order: in fact the pontiff especially forbids the bishops and other ecclesiastics to hinder the Franciscans in this jurisdiction which he accords them.

Other decrees of the Holy See favor the jurisdiction of the Friars Minor in the same manner.[84] When some of the Tertiaries received permission to establish community life, their Superiors (Third Order Regular) in Spain, Portugal and the West Indies were given jurisdiction over the Secular Tertiaries.[85]

At the time that the Friars Minor Capuchin received their papal approbation, they were given jurisdiction over the secular Tertiaries in the same manner as that enjoyed by the other Franciscan Families when Clement VII granted them 'all the privileges which have been accorded to the Friars Minor';[86] their jurisdiction and also that of the Third Order Regular was repeated by Clement X, February 16, 1676.[87]

It was but natural that the authority of receiving into the

[83] Sixtus IV, Bull, *Romani Pontificis*, Dec. 15, 1471 (*Orbis Seraphicus*, II, 893-895).

[84] Sixtus IV, Oct. 16, 1477 (*Orbis Seraphicus*, II, 895 f); Innocent VIII, Apr. 5, 1492 (*o. c.*, 896 f); Alexander VI, Aug. 26, 1492 (*o. c.*, 897 f); Julius II, Oct. 15, 1507 (*o. c.*, 898-900).

[85] Paul III, *Ad uberes fructus*, 1547 (Wadding, *Annales Minorum*, XVIII, 435-460).

[86] Bull, *Religionis zelus*, July 4, 1528, § IX (*Bull. Capuc.*, I, p. 3).

[87] Bull, *Sollicitudo pastoralis* (*o. c.*, p. 125 f).

Third Order was gradually taken from the Tertiaries themselves and transferred to the Friars Minor, in proportion as their control over the Tertiaries grew more pronounced. The Rule of Nicholas IV in 1289 allows Tertiary officials to receive postulants into the Order (Chap. II), but the Statutes of the Third Order Secular approved at the Friars Minor General Chapter in 1688[38] gives this authority to the Guardian (ad Cap. XVI). The right of the Friars Minor in this regard became so inviolable that in the eighteenth century the Congregation of Bishops and Regulars declared that professions made in the hands of Tertiaries were invalid, and at the same time granted a sanation in favor of past professions made in this manner.[39]

Since Nicholas IV had transferred the obligation and privilege of visitation from the ordinaries of the places to the Friars Minor, it is evident that the bishops had little or nothing to do with the spiritual welfare of the Tertiaries *as Tertiaries*. Hence this pontiff implicitly reduced the authority of the ordinaries of the places to that of vigilance over the funds of Tertiary sodalities or fraternities and to the proper conduct of divine services, as was later specifically mentioned by the Council of Trent.[40]

Toward the end of the seventeenth century this was true, not only of Tertiary Sodalities erected in the Churches of the Friars Minor, but also in those places where there were no Franciscan Religious foundations.[41]

[38] The statutes had papal approbation; for their history cf. below chap. VIII, Art. I.

[39] June 18, 1717, ad III-IV (*Fontes*, n. 1834).

[40] Sess. XXII, *de reformat.*, cap. 8.

[41] The *Statuta Innocentiana*, ad cap. XVI, has the following: "Itaque *in pagis* poterunt fratres, et sorores sollicitare, ut aliquis sacerdos petat a p. Guardiano suam authoritatem, in ordine ad illis assistendum, sicut assistit Visitator religiosus in Civitatibus ubi sunt Conventus. Poterunt similiter facere suas Congregationes, et electiones officiorum. Nihi-

At this time, the three branches of the First Order, as well as the Third Order Regular, enjoyed jurisdiction over the Secular Tertiaries. There is nothing to indicate that the consent of the ordinary of the place was required for the valid or licit erection of Third Order Sodalities.

II Period

From Pope Benedict XIII to the Promulgation of the Code of Canon Law

When Sixtus IV subjected the Secular Tertiaries to the authority of the Friars Minor, he gave authority to the Minister-General of the Conventuals, and the Vicar-General of the Observant Family. However, during the time of Leo X, conditions were reversed, not that the authority over the Tertiaries was changed in any way, but the Minister-General of the Observant Family was given the place of precedence.[43]

Thus it came about in 1725 that Pope Benedict XIII—whose papal pronouncements may in truth be considered the most important and far-reaching in the history of the Third Order—in repeating the subjection of the Tertiaries to the Friars Minor, addressed this entire authority to the Minister-General of the Observant Family, *apparently* ex-

lominus ad Visitatorem Religiosum pertinet semper singulis annis visitare fraternitates Tertii Ordinis, quae fuerint per totam Guardianiam, si ipse Guardianus nolit facere". Cf. for example the decisions of the Congregation of Bishops and Regulars which in all cases that can be applied to the Third Order Secular, limit the jurisdiction of the Ordinary of the place to that of vigilance over the funds and the proper conduct of divine cult as decreed in the Council of Trent: Aug. 2, 1581 (*Fontes*, n. 1387); June 12, 1582 (*o. c.*, n. 1396); 1589 (*o. c.*, n. 1421); Feb. 22, 1595 (*o. c.*, n. 1533); Sept. 7, 1598 (*o. c.*, n. 1573); Feb. 3, 1610 (*o. c.*, n. 1647); June 9, 1617 (*o. c.*, n. 1690); July 21, 1617 (*o. c.*, n. 1691); July 31, 1637 (*o. c.*, n. 1752); Oct. 5, 1646 (*o. c.*, n. 1780).

[43] Bull, *Ite et Vos,* May 29, 1517 (*Bull. Rom.*, V, 692-698).

cluding the other Friars Minor from any jurisdiction, except with his permission. It pertains to him to garb with the habit, receive profession, erect Third Order Sodalities, and perform the canonical visitation.[44] He is to propagate the Third Order by erecting Sodalities everywhere (§8), and where Sodalities have already been erected, another cannot be located without his permission, under pain of invalidity (§9). He is empowered to enact statutes, and in fact to change anything in regard to the Third Order which he may consider in the interest of its spiritual welfare, and which is not against the Rule (§8). Obedience to the Franciscan Superiors alone, is demanded of the Tertiaries in all things which pertain to the Rule, and in all controversies: expulsion by the Franciscan Superiors is to be the penalty of disobedience.[45]

The most important point of this constitution is that the ordinary of the place is entirely and expressly excluded from any of these points of jurisdiction which have been enumerated.[46]

Thus: a) the jurisdiction of the Friars Minor is supreme to the exclusion of all others; b) Third Order Sodalities are bound by the *lex loci* as contained today in canon 711 §1, but from which the Minister-General may dispense; (§9) c) since the ordinary of the place is positively excluded from all jurisdiction, he has no right to perform the canonical visitation in regard to the temporalities of the Tertiaries even in those Sodalities erected outside of Franciscan Churches; but where Tertiaries are located in a church or

[44] Bull, *Paterna Sedis Apostolicae*, Dec. 10, 1725 (*Bull. Rom.*, XXII, 285-294).

[45] § 7; "ad cassationem usque * * * habitus * * *," (§ 8).

[46] "* * * privative quoad alios quoscumque * * *"; and that there may be no mistake, the ordinary of the place is specifically excluded: "* * * seclusis locorum ordinariis et aliis quibuscumque personis cujusve status * * *". (§ 8).

chapel which belongs properly to themselves, the ordinary of the place retains the right of visitation in reference to the altar and to the proper conduct of divine cult.[47]

But the same pontiff on account of discordances which naturally arose due to this apparent exclusive subjection of the Tertiaries to the Friars Minor Observant, and because of the injustice which the other Franciscan Families felt themselves to have incurred, reaffirmed in favor of the Friars Minor Capuchin that jurisdiction which they had possessed before, so that they could erect Sodalities of Tertiaries, receive profession, instruct in the Rule, and provide for the spiritual welfare of the Tertiaries. Contrary to the declaration of the preceding Bull, they may erect in any place, even where others have already been founded.[48]

For the same reasons, two weeks later Benedict XIII gave to the Minister-General of the Friars Minor Conventual all jurisdiction which had ever been accorded to him by former papal decrees; it was to be the same as that given in the Bull, *Paterna Sedis Apostolicae,* Dec. 10, 1725, to the Friars Minor Observant; he also abolished the lex loci.[49] That there would be no misunderstanding, he repeated the jurisdiction of the Friars Minor Conventual a second time, and at the same time gave additional reasons.[50]

It is interesting to note that the Bull, *Paterna Sedis Apostolicae,* (quoted above as giving jurisdiction to the Friars

[47] Council of Trent, Sess. XXII, *de reformat.*, cap 8.

[48] Bull, *Ratio Apostolici Ministerii,* June 23, 1726 (*Bull. Rom.*, XXII, 367-370).

[49] Bull, *Singularis Devotio,* July 5, 1726 (*o. c.*, 370-373).

[50] "Etenim equum est ut ministro generali Ordinis * * * Conventualium B. Francisci, qui inter caeteros Ordines, sub uno et eodem Seraphico patre et capite Deo famulantes, vetustissimus est, omnem jurisdictionem, auctoritatem, facultates et gratias in Tertii Ordinis, ab eodem celeberrimo confessore instituti, poenitentes indulgeamus, quae aliis fratribus Minoribus indultae fuerunt * * *" (§ 5).

Minor Observant) was understood at the time of its promulgation as giving *exclusive* jurisdiction to the Friars Minor *Observant,* to the extreme that the other Families possessed no jurisdiction whatsoever; this is proven from the fact that dissensions arose as is mentioned in the two subsequent Bulls of the same pontiff, which gave jurisdiction to the Friars Minor Capuchin and Conventual as noted above. But the pontiff deplores this in these latter decrees: (*Ratio Apostolici Ministerii,* §1)—"* * * litteras * * * perperam *detortas* fuisse intelleximus; * * * Tertiarii Cappucini * * * Minoribus a regulari observantia nuncupatis *nullo modo* subsunt; sed ministri generali * * * Minorum * * * qui Cappucini appelantur, * * *". (Signularis Devotio, §1)—"Hanc * * * constitutionem [Paterna Sedis Apostolicae] * * * contra expressam mentem nostram, * * * *detortam* fuisse intelleximus".

He thus states expressly that he did not wish to deprive the Friars Minor *Capuchin* and *Conventual* of jurisdiction over the Tertiaries. In the Bull, *Paterna Sedis Apostolicae,* the words *'de Observantia',* are not used but rather the simple words *'ministri generali totius Ordinis'.* Doubtless it was understood as comprising only the *Observant* Family, because Leo X, May 29, 1517, by the Bull, *Ite et vos,*[51] had given the General of the *Observants* the title *'Minister Generalis Ordinis Minorum',* and also the place of precedence. Ferraris, without taking into consideration the words of Benedict XIII in his *subsequent* Bulls, quotes the Bull, *Paterna Sedis Apostolicae,* as being in favor of the Friars Minor *Observant,* and as *excluding* the Friars Minor Capuchin and Conventual from any jurisdiction over the Tertiaries.[52] Hilarius Parisiensis,[53] makes no comment in this particular regard in quoting these Bulls.

Despite the misleading words of Ferraris, the words of Benedict XIII are clear: by the Bull, *Paterna Sedis Apostolicae,* he did not suppress the jurisdiction of the Friars Minor *Capuchin* and *Conventual*—he only gave the *Observant* Family more privileges than the other two families enjoyed, but which he subsequently extended to them.

[51] *Bull. Rom.,* V, 692-698.
[52] Ferraris, *s. v. Tertiarii,* n. 26.
[53] *Liber Tertii Ordinis,* p. 228-237.

These three Bulls were again confirmed in 1728, with the additional ruling that Tertiaries are not allowed to transfer from one Franciscan Family to another; the *lex loci* as laid down in the constitution, *Paterna Sedis Apostolicae,* was again to be enforced.[64] This last prescription was again abolished when Clement XII reaffirmed the jurisdiction of the Friars Minor Capuchin over the Tertiaries;[65] it has not been subsequently revived.

The Third Order Regular also enjoys the same privileges and rights toward the Secular Tertiaries, as was given to the Friars Minor Observant by the Bull, *Paterna Sedis Apostolicae.*[66] Pope Benedict XIV implicitly reaffirmed the jurisdiction of the four Franciscan Families when he granted a number of indulgences and privileges 'to the Brothers and Sisters of the Third Order Secular of Penance, under the care and direction of any Regular Order of St. Francis'.[67]

There have been no changes in regara to the subjection of the Tertiaries to the Franciscan Religious, and therefore this point may rest with advantage by quoting the words of Pope Leo XIII in his Rule for the Third Order Secular of St. Francis: "The visitors[68] shall be chosen from the First

[64] Benedict XIII, Bull, *Dilecti filii,* July 22, 1728 (Ferraris, *s. v. Religiones Regulares,* Art. 5, n. 55: he quotes the Constitution in full; *s. v. Tertiarii,* n. 29, the date is given as June 21, 1728).

[65] Bull, *Apostolicae servitutis,* July 23, 1735 (*Bull. Rom.*, XXIV, 61 f).

[66] Benedict XIII, Bull, *Exponi Nobis,* Sept. 30, 1729 (*Bull. Rom.*, XXII, 856-858).

[67] Bull, *Ad Romanum Pontificem,* March 15, 1751 (*Bull. Rom. Continuatio,* III, 285, § 5).

[68] The term *'visitor'* is not limited merely to the one who performs the annual canonical visitation, but also embraces that Franciscan official who has the care and direction of a Third Order Sodality; cf. the *Rule of Leo XIII* (*Fontes,* n. 588), and the *Ceremonial of the Third Order Secular of St. Francis,* approved by the same pontiff and the S. C. of Rites June 18, 1883 (Fleming, *Leonis XIII Acta ad III Ordinem Spectantia,* p. 197-222).

Order or the Third Order Regular". (*Rule,* III §3).

It is not to be forgotten, however, that the secular clergy have exercised great influence over the Third Order. During its early existence it was the diocesan bishop who performed the canonical visitation, and even in the Rule of Nicholas IV in 1289, he only counseled (*consulimus*) that the visitors and informers (*informatores*) be taken from the Friars Minor. In the very first Rule of the Third Order there is provision made for clerics.[59] Many of the secular clergy were influential in sustaining the existence of the institution where there were no Franciscan Religious.[60]

The Statutes of Innocent XI make mention of this fact when they state that "in isolated localities (*in pagis*) the brethren and sisters of the Third Order may apply to a secular priest to obtain from the Father Guardian [Friar Minor] the power to take such care of them as is done by the religious visitor. They may likewise conduct the meetings and arrange for the election of the various officers. Still the right of the annual visitation is reserved to the religious visitor".[61]

Leo XIII in more recent times recommended to all the bishops, especially to those of Italy, that they apply to the Franciscan Superiors for faculties to invest in the Third Order.[62] Pius X also expressed the desire that the Third Order be established not only at the monasteries and churches of the Franciscan religious, but also in parishes under the care of the secular clergy, who should apply, with the approval of the bishop, to the Franciscan Superiors for faculties; however the right of the Franciscan Superiors

[59] *Regula Antiqua,* V, 2.
[60] Callaey, *The Third Order of St. Francis,* p. 39-46.
[61] Ad Cap. XVI.
[62] Encyclical, *Auspicato,* Sept. 7, 1882 (*A. S. S.,* XV, 145-153).

must always be borne in mind.[63] Benedict XV also expressed the same wish when he recommended that the Third Order be spread everywhere.[64]

Appendix to Article II

Concerning the Revocation of the Benedictine Constitutions giving Jurisdiction to the Friars Minor

A great number of Constitutions given out by authority of Benedict XIII throughout were revoked at least in part by his successor, Clement XII, March 29, 1732.[65]

Among the Bulls which he specifically mentions, are those by which Benedict XIII had completely subjected the Franciscan Tertiaries to the jurisdiction of the four Franciscan Families, to the exclusion of the ordinaries of the places, and which have been quoted throughout this article as having the force of law. Hence the importance of discovering the mind of Clement XII and of consequently determining which juridical points of the Benedictine constitutions he wished to abolish; which points he wished to retain the force of law.

The four constitutions of Benedict XIII giving jurisdiction to the Franciscans which are mentioned in the Bull of revocation are: *Paterna Sedis Apostolicae,* Dec. 10, 1725, in favor of the Friars Minor Observant,[66] *Ratio Apostolica Ministerii,* June 23, 1726, in favor of the Friars Minor Capu-

[63] Const., *Tertium Franciscalium Ordinem,* Sept. 8, 1912 (*A. A. S.,* IV [1912], 584 f).

[64] Encyclical, *Sacra Propediem,* Jan. 6, 1921 (*A. A. S.,* XIII [1921], 33-41).

[65] Bull, *Romanus Pontifex* (*Bull. Rom.,* 323-327); the complete list coming under this revocation is given in § 1 of this Bull.

[66] *Bull. Rom.,* XXII, 285-294.

chin,[67] *Singularis devotio,* July 5, 1726, in favor of the Friars Minor Conventual,[68] *Exponi nobis,* Sept. 30, 1729, in favor of the Third Order Regular.[69] There were also others mentioned in the revocation which concerned the privileges granted to various religious organizations, and which will be used here to prove that the revocation was not in whole, but rather only in part. At first sight it would appear that Clement XII had completely *abolished* all the Benedictine constitutions which he mentions in the revocation, for he uses the words: *ac si constitutiones illae non emanassent;*[70] but from the subsequent practice of the Holy See and the opinions of prominent authors it can be seen that he revoked them only *in part,* namely in those things which tended to foment dissension and which impeded the jurisdiction of the bishops, regarding not *Secular* Tertiaries, but rather concerning those who lived *collegiately,* and also those who lived a *quasi-religious life in their homes* whom Benedict XIII had placed under the complete jurisdiction of the Friars Minor, *'exclusis locorum ordinariis'.*[71]

In order to prove that the force of the Constitutions of Benedict XIII regarding the jurisdiction of the Franciscans over the *Secular* Tertiaries was not lost or abolished through the revocation of Clement XII, a three-fold argument will be used:

A) The Benedictine Constitutions mentioned by Clement XIII were not revoked in whole. B) The revocation of Clement XII had special reference to the juridical subjection of collegiate Tertiaries and of women who lived a quasi-religious life in their homes whom Benedict XIII had freed from the jurisdiction of

[67] *O. c.,* 367-370.
[68] *O. c.,* 370-373.
[69] *O. c.,* 856-858.
[70] § 2 of the Bull of revocation.
[71] Cf. for example the Bull, *Paterna Sedis Apostolicae,* in favor of the Friars Minor Observant (*o. c.* 289 § 8) where these words are used.

the bishops and placed entirely under the care of the religious Orders. C) The revocation of Clement XII did not affect the jurisdiction which Benedict XIII had conceded to the Friars Minor over the Secular Tertiaries.

A) The Benedictine Constitutions mentioned by Clement XII were not revoked in whole:

The following decisions of the Holy See indicate this:

The Order of Canonical Regulars of the Holy Redeemer, having been conceded many indulgences and privileges by Benedict XIII in his constitution, *In Sede,* March 26, 1729 (which was mentioned in the revocation), requested of the S. Congregation of Indulgences whether these privileges were revoked by Clement XII, using in the petition the argument in their favor that '*only those privileges which were contentious*' were revoked. The following question was asked: *"An per moderationem seu revocationem expressam Bullae* [*In Sede*] *favore Regularium editae Indulgentiae ipsis a Benedicto XIII concessae, necnon privilegium altaris intelligatur revocatum"*? Response: *"Negative"*.[72]

Another Bull which came under the revocation of Clement XII was *Pretiosus,*[73] concerning privileged altars which he had extended under certain conditions to Chapels of the Confraternity of the Rosary; being asked whether the altar was also privileged in regard to deceased brethren, the Congregation of Indulgences replied in the negative; but it did not give this reply because the privilege of Benedict XIII was revoked, but 'quia recensitum privilegium * * * a s. m. Benedicto XIII ad quaecumque altare Rosarii extensum, tantummodo privilegium personale *est*'.[74] Therefore this privilege *is* in force despite the revocation of Clement XII.

The same argument may be used from the words of Leo

[72] Jan. 23, 1733 (*Decreta Authentica S. C. Indulg.*, n. 105).

[73] May 25, 1725 (*Bull. Rom.*, XXII, 552-554).

[74] Nov. 27, 1764 (*Decreta Authentica S. C. Indulg.*, n. 233).

XIII[75] who states that he revokes certain privileges granted to the Friars Preachers by Benedict XIII;[76] the privilege which he revoked had been given in the Bull Pretiosus which was mentioned by Clement XII in his revocation; since Leo XIII cannot revoke that which had already been revoked by Clement XII, it necessarily follows that *he did not consider the revocation of Clement XII to have abolished this particular privilege. Therefore the Bull, Pretiosus, was not entirely revoked by Clement XII.*

Similar force can also be deduced from the words of the Congregation of Indulgences approving a list of Indulgences for the Archconfraternity of the Rosary: *"Pius IX confirmed all the indulgences granted by his predecessors which are herein accurately transcribed"*.[77] One of the Indulgences which he thus confirmed[78] is taken from this same Bull, *Pretiosus* §5. Arguing from the words of the Congregation it is clear that Pius IX did not *grant* these indulgences, but rather *confirmed them as already having force* due to their concession by his predecessors.

In a dispute between the Franciscan Tertiaries of Valletta and the Friars Minor Observant,[79] the latter denied the right of the former to march in the same procession under the cross of the religious.[80] The Tertiaries appealed to the Congregation of Bishops and Regulars, citing in their favor[81] the Bull, *Paterna Sedis Apostolicae* of Benedict XIII, Dec. 10, 1725, §X;[82] this is one of the principal Bulls giving jurisdic-

[75] Const. *Ubi primum*, Oct. 10, 1898 (*A. S. S.*, XXXI, 257-263).

[76] In the above-mentioned Bull, *Pretiosus*, § 4.

[77] *S. C. of Indulg.*, Sept. 18, 1862 (*Rescripta Authentica S. C. Indulg.*, p. 427).

[78] *O. c.*, p. 421.

[79] *A. S. S.*, XXVI, 485-498.

[80] *O. c.*, 485 f.

[81] *O. c.*, 491.

[82] The *Bull. Rom.*, XXII, 290, cites this privilege under § IX.

tion to the Friars Minor over the Tertiaries. The rights of the Tertiaries were upheld by the Congregation Aug. 25, 1893,[83] thereby implying that despite the revocation of Clement XII, this Bull still retained its vigor, at least in this regard. These decisions are sufficient to prove that Clement XII did not *entirely* revoke the Constitutions of Benedict XIII which he gives in his list.

B) The revocation of Clement XII had special reference to the juridical subjection of collegiate Tertiaries and of women who lived a quasi-religious life in their homes whom Benedict XIII had freed from the jurisdiction of the bishops and placed entirely under the care of the Religious Orders:

Clement XII desired to return that jurisdiction to the bishops which Benedict XIII had given to the Regulars in regard to the *collegiate* Tertiaries. The latter had declared that not only all *secular,* but also all *collegiate* Franciscan Tertiaries who did not place themselves under the jurisdiction of the Friars Minor to the exclusion of the bishops, were to be deprived of all indulgences and privileges.[84] Thus in 1736 such (collegiate) Tertiaries asked the S. C. of Indulgences whether, notwithstanding the fact that they were now under the jurisdiction of the bishops, they still partook of the indulgences and privileges of the Order; the Congregation replied in the affirmative,[85] evidently taking into consideration that Clement XII had returned the *collegiate* Tertiaries to the jurisdiction of the bishops when he revoked the Constitutions of Benedict XIII.

Benedict XIV in treating this question, exhibits decrees of the Congregation of Bishops and Regulars which very clearly demonstrate that the questions involved were those regarding whether *collegiate* Tertiaries were subject to the

[83] Ad II (*A. S. S.*, XXVI, 497 f).
[84] E. g. in the Bull, *Paterna Sedis Apostolicae,* Dec. 10, 1725.
[85] Dec. 3, 1736 (*Decreta Authentica S. C. Indulg.*, n. 118).

Regular Orders or to the Bishops.[86] He then goes on to explain that if nothing had been changed after the Constitutions of Benedict XIII, the bishops would surely enjoy no jurisdiction over these collegiate Tertiaries; but since the Bull, *Romanus Pontifex* of Clement XII revoked the rights of the Friars Minor in this regard, '*res tota ad eos limites restituenda est, quibus ante Benedictinum XIII. concludebatur, et quos antea recensuimus.*[87] *Unde redditur Episcopo pristina auctoritas, quam in has* [*collegiatas*] *Tertiarias exercebat, et ob hanc causam ipsis Sacram Visitationem indiximus*'.[88]

The S. C. of the Propagation of the Faith in an instruction given 1763, quotes these words of Benedict XIV[89] and expressly states that the revocation of Clement XII had reference to those Tertiaries as mentioned above.[90]

The same is true of the canonist Ferraris, who after declaring that the *Collegiate* Tertiaries were subjected to the jurisdiction of the Franciscans and the Dominicans to the

[86] *Institutiones Ecclesiasticae*, CV, LXXVIII in particular; the entire Article § II, beginning with LXXIII indicates this.

[87] *O. c.*, LXXIX; he gives the former status in the numbers immediately preceding.

[88] *O. c.*, LXXX.

[89] The Instruction quotes the *Institutes* as 105, 76; the edition of Rome 1785 and Prati 1884 of the *Institutes* quotes these words of Benedict XIV under 105, 80, with slightly different wording than that given in the Instruction; the meaning however is the same.

[90] *Collectanea S. C. de Prop. F.*, n. 448; that the Tertiaries concerning whom the Instruction speaks are not Franciscan Secular Tertiaries is very clear from the words of the Congregation concerning the conditions of membership: "* * * ac in aetate saltem quadraginta annorum constitutas, quae de proprio habent unde sufficienter vivere possint, et non cum aliis viris quam consanguineis, vel affinibus in primo tantum gradu sibi conjunctis cohabitent, et ab Ordinario loci prius licentia impetrata, qui non aliter eam concedat, nisi de praedictis examine diligenti sibi constiterit". There never was such a condition of membership in the Third Order Secular of St. Francis.

exclusion of the bishops, by the Constitutions of Benedict XIII,[91] adds, that now, due to the Constitution *Romanus Pontifex* of Clement XII, the bishops enjoy the same authority over these collegiate Tertiaries as they possessed before the Benedictine Constitutions.[92]

C) The revocation of Clement XII did not affect the jurisdiction which Benedict XIII had conceded to the Friars Minor over the Secular Tertiaries:

Although not expressly mentioned, this is clearly insinuated by the Instruction of the Congregation of the Propagation of the Faith mentioned above. In its preliminary remarks, the Congregation mentions that serious dissensions have arisen regarding the respective rights of the bishops and the regulars over these Tertiaries, 'because the Apostolic Constitutions have not been fully known and clearly understood on this point'.[93] The Instruction then follows and demonstrates that the Constitution *Romanus Pontifex* of Clement XII returned that jurisdiction to the bishops over *Collegiate* Tertiaries and those who lived a quasi-religious life in their homes (the description of which is given above, note 90), which they had enjoyed before the Benedictine Constitutions. The Instruction does not even touch on the question of secular Tertiaries. If the Clementine Constitution had abrogated the rights conceded by Benedict XIII to the Friars Minor over the *Secular,* as well as the *Collegiate,* Tertiaries, the Sacred Congregation, treating the question of jurisdiction *ex professo,* would without doubt

[91] Ferraris, *s. v. Tertiarii,* n. 52.

[92] "Unde, ut vides, et recte tradit Bened. XIV, volum. V. notificat. 17, § 2, redit in pristinum jurisdictio ordinariorum supra Tertiarias *collegialiter* viventes, ac si minime emanassent dictae Benedictinae Constitutiones, * * *" (*o. c.,* n. 54).

[93] " * * * quod Pontificum Constitutiones omnes hac de re non satis sint notae, ac privilegia a Sede Apostolica Tertio Ordini concessa non probe intelligantur".

have decided that the rights of the Friars Minor over the former as well as the latter, were lost by the revocation of Clement XII. Were this revocation universal, the Congregation could the more easily have decided the question by simply stating that the jurisdiction of the bishops over *all* Tertiaries is the same as it was before the Benedictine Constitutions; but by distinguishing between the two and mentioning this change of jurisdiction only of the *Collegiate* Tertiaries (whose conditions of membership it describes in detail in order to make itself clear) the logical conclusion is that the status of the Secular Tertiaries was not changed by Clement XII. The same argument may be applied to the Institutes of Benedict XIV quoted above.

Ferraris is still more clear on this point. He quotes the four Constitutions of Benedict XIII as giving jurisdiction to the Friars Minor over the *Secular* Tertiaries, particularly that given in favor of the Observant Family of the Order (Paterna Sedis Apostolicae) which he quotes verbatim because it contains the basic elements of all four Constitutions.[94] He adds nothing here concerning their revocation, thereby attributing to them the force of law, in his opinion. But when he goes over to the treatment of *Collegiate* Tertiaries he prohibits the use of these same Constitutions and the Constitution, *Pretiosus,*[95] as having value concerning the jurisdiction of Regulars over *Collegiate* Tertiaries, because these Constitutions together with others, have been reduced to the terms of common law by Clement XII,[96] and therefore 'redit in pristinum jurisdictio ordinariorum locorum supra Tertiarias *Collegialiter* viventes, ac si minime emanassent

[94] Ferraris, *s. v. Tertiarii,* nn. 26-35.

[95] May 25, 1727, in favor of the Friars Preachers (*Bull. Rom.,* XXII, 522-554).

[96] Ferraris, *s. v. Tertiarii,* nn. 52-54.

dictae Benedictinae constitutiones eas a tali jurisdictone eximentes'."[97]

In two instances Clement XII himself implies that the points of the Benedictine Constitutions giving jurisdiction to the Friars Minor over the *Secular* Tertiaries remain intact despite his own revocation—1) Upon the request of the Minister-General of the Friars Minor Capuchin he declared that the Capuchins are legitimate sons of St. Francis and therefore enjoy the right of receiving into the Third Order, and the Tertiaries whom they receive enjoy the same privileges as others, no matter upon what Minister-General they are *dependent* (a quocumque ministro generali dependentium).[98] It was in fact through the Benedictine Constitutions that the Tertiaries were placed in a state of *dependence* on the Friars Minor to the exclusion of the ordinaries of the places. b) In the list of Bulls which he mentions as coming under his revocation he cites the four giving such jurisdiction to the Franciscans,[99] but he fails to name a fifth, *Dilecti Filii,* June 21, 1728[100] which confirms these four explicitly regarding the jurisdiction of the Franciscans over the Secular Tertiaries; from which the conclusion must necessarily be drawn that he desired this jurisdiction to retain its force.

The Congregation of Bishops and Regulars in a dispute between the Friars Minor and a local ordinary (episcopus Narniensis), implicitly affirmed this jurisdiction as given by Benedict XIII, when, being asked whether the former may receive into the Third Order *'irrequisito Ordinario',* it re-

[97] *O. c.*, n. 54.

[98] Bull, *Apostolicae Servitutis,* July 23, 1735 (*Bull. Rom.*, XXIV, 61 f).

[99] Cf. above: the beginning of this appendix.

[100] The pars dispositiva of this Bull is given in Ferraris, *o. c.*, n. 29.

plied in the affirmative (affirmative, absque tamen ulla exemptione).[101]

The question is definitely settled by a decision of the same Congregation in 1740. In a dispute between the Friars Minor *Observant* and the Friars Minor *Discalced,* the former contended that the latter had no rights of jurisdiction over the Secular Tertiaries. In its decree on the question the Congregation admonishes that all legitimate sons of St. Francis, no matter by what name they may be called, partake of the jurisdiction *which was accorded to all Franciscans by the Apostolic Constitutions of Benedict XIII and Clement XII.*[102] *'Therefore there is no reason why the Discalced Friars Minor cannot use this same privilege, since they are legitimate sons of St. Francis, * * * and the Congregation defines it in this manner'.*[103] Benedict XIV approved this decree and embodied it in his Constitution, *Laudabile,* Aug. 2, 1745.[104] Neither can it be said that the Congregation is *reviving* the Benedictine Constitutions, for the context of the decision indicates beyond a doubt that the Congregation considered this jurisdiction as granted by Benedict XIII to be in existence at the time of the dispute, even before the decision was rendered.

The weight of authors who cite one or more of the Constitutions of Benedict XIII in order to prove the present status of the Secular Tertiaries of St. Francis, may also be cited as a proof.[105]

[101] Sept. 5, 1738 (Ferraris, *o. c.,* n. 51).

[102] The latter is the Bull of Clement XII repeating the jurisdiction of the Friars Minor Capuchin as given above note 98.

[103] *S. C. of Bishops and Regulars,* Sept. 11, 1740 (*Bull. Rom. Continuatio,* I, 548 f).

[104] *O. c.,* 547-550.

[105] Vermeersch, *De Religiosis Institutis et Personis,* I, n. 536; Piat, *Praelectiones Juris Regularis,* II, Q. 71; Ferreres, *Institutiones Canonicae,* I, n. 976; Ferraris, *s. v. Tertiarii;* Ojetti, *Synopsis Rerum*

Conclusion: The Benedictine Constitutions had given complete jurisdiction to the Regular Orders over both Collegiate and Secular Tertiaries, to the exclusion of the ordinaries of the places. Clement XII revoked the rights of the Regulars over the Collegiate, but did not change the status of the Secular Tertiaries. Therefore the Constitutions of Benedict XIII have juridical value as regards the authority of the Friars Minor over the Third Order Secular of St. Francis.

Article III

Pre-Code Legal Status of the Order In the Eyes of the Church.

Exemptions.

Since the feudal system in the middle ages was abused to a great extent and therefore the oath of fealty was often the cause of much oppression of the poor, Honorius III realized that this close affiliation and relation of the Tertiaries with the secular powers would be a great stumbling block to them in the attainment of their spiritual and material ends: the acquirement of perfection and the alleviation of the sufferings of the sick, the poor and the dying as prescribed in their Rule.[1] He therefore freed the Tertiaries of Fienza from three important obligations—that of a) bearing arms; b)

Moralium et Juris Pontificii, s. v. Tertiarii; Antonius de Cipressa, *Regula sive Modus Vivendi Fratrum de Poenitentia S. Francisci,* p. 36-43; Mocchegiani, *Collectio Indulgentiarum,* n. 1529; Mocchegiani, *Jurisprudentia Ecclesiastica,* II, n. 675; Hilarius Parisiensis, *Liber Tertii Ordinis,* p. 228-237; Mileta, *Trattato giuridico sul Terz' Ordine Secolare,* p. 47; Tachy, *Les Tiers Ordres,* p. 5 f; Tischler, *Handbuch zur Leitung des Dritten Ordens,* p. 55; Holzapfel, *Die Leitung des Dritten Ordens,* p. 68-79; Stein, *Tertius Ordo Francoscalis,* p. 43-46.

[1] Cf. *Third Order Forum,* I [1922], p. 21.

doing military service; c) taking oaths;[2] at this time he also implicitly confirmed the Third Order. In 1228 Gregory IX confirmed the Bull of his predecessor when he issued a decree in their favor. However, since it was necessary for the brethren to take oaths at times, he made the following exceptions to the Rule Bull of Honorius III: the Tertiaries could take an oath—to preserve peace; to maintain the faith; to clear themselves of a calumny, and to bear witness in court.[3] By this Bull Gregory IX extends to the Tertiaries of entire Italy, the favors formerly granted by Honorius III and himself to particular groups of Tertiaries. This was again confirmed by Innocent IV in 1252.[4]

However, since the faithful flocked to the standard of the Order in such great numbers, the privilege of not bearing arms had to be mitigated. Therefore in the Rule published by Nicholas IV in his Bull, *Supra montem* (1289), he allows the Tertiaries to bear arms 'in the defense of one's country, of the Church, for the faith of Christ, and for a reason approved by the ministers.'[5] This Bull is the solemn approval of the Order; it also repeats the legislation of Gregory IX regarding the taking of oaths, with the exception that they may be taken for reason of 'contractu emptionis, venditionis, et donationis.'[6]

Another important privilege of the Tertiaries was that

[2] Bull, *Significatum est nobis,* Dec. 16, 1221 (*Bull. Franc.,* I, n. 8, p. 8).

[3] Bull, *Detestanda,* March 30, 1228 (*o. c.,* n. 20, p. 39 f); the prescription of this Bull is contained in the *Regula Antiqua,* V, 4; but since in 1221 (when the first Rule was written) Honorius III decreed that they should *not* take an oath, it follows that this part was not added to the original Rule till the year 1228.

[4] Bull, *Detestanda,* Apr. 11, 1252 (*Bull. Franc. Epitome,* n. 609a); this is merely a repetition of the Bull, *Detestanda,* of Gregory IX.

[5] Cap. VII.

[6] Cap. XII.

they were not obliged to accept public office; this was granted by Gregory IX and was repeated in after years.[7] The fact that the Tertiaries were exempt from taking oaths except in particular cases allowed by the Rule, gave them the exemption of being cited not in a civil, but in an ecclesiastical court before the bishop: the *privilegium fori.*[8] This was certainly an important privilege to be granted to lay persons and is evidence of the high esteem in which the Third Order was held by the Holy See. The Tertiaries were to pay their legitimate taxes but were excused from them if they were unjust [9]—a great blow to the extreme burdens which at times were placed upon the shoulders of the poorer classes. Devotion to, and faith in, the Church and its legitimate representatives were always the keynotes in the lives of the Tertiaries; the bishops were to stop vexations by the local lords;[10] postulants were to be purged from the suspicion of heresy by him before being allowed to enter the Order;[11] a Friar Minor was to be called to settle disputes among the brethren.[12]

In fact, so great was the standing of the Tertiaries in the eyes of the Church that Pope Sixtus IV, following the opinion of canonists of that time, went so far as to consider them

[7] Bull, *Nimis patenter,* June 25, 1227 (*Bull. Franc.,* I, n. 7, p. 30 f); *Cum dilecti,* June 4, 1230 (*o. c.,* n. 53, p. 65 f); *Nimis Patenter,* Apr. 5, 1231 (*o. c.,* n. 69, p. 71); *Ne is,* March 15, 1233 (*o. c.,* n. 94, p. 99); Alexander V, *Pia desideria,* Apr. 27, 1255 (*o. c.,* II, n. 50, p. 42).

[8] *Regula Antiqua,* X, 3; XIII, 13; Pope Celestine V confirmed this by the Bull, *Desideriis vestris,* Sept. 2, 1294 (*Bull. Franc.,* IV, n. 2, p. 330; cf. also *o. c.,* n. 3).

[9] Gregory IX, Bull, *Nimis patenter,* June 25, 1227 (*Bull. Franc.,* I, n. 7, p. 30 f); also by the Bull, *Detestanda,* of the same pope, March 30, 1228 (*o. c.,* n. 20, p. 39 f).

[10] *Regula Antiqua,* X, 2-3.

[11] *O. c.,* XI, 1.

[12] *A. F. H.,* I [1908], p. 549, n. X.

as ecclesiastical persons with all their rights.[13] Six years later he extended this still farther by declaring that the Tertiaries of both Franciscans and Dominicans had all the material and spiritual privileges of both First Orders, no matter what they may be.[14]

The ownership and property rights of a legitimately organized group of Tertiaries could not be infringed upon after the fraternity had once been canonically established. At times the civil rulers attempted to seize these goods, but were reprimanded by the Holy See; thus in 1228 Gregory IX denounced the civil magistrates who attempted to prevent the Tertiaries from distributing their goods among the poor.[15] Nicholas IV also remonstrated with the bishop of Florence, who attempted the same injustice against the Tertiaries.[16]

A commendable fact in favor of the Tertiaries was that, notwithstanding their immunity from accepting public office, the civil authorities often attempted to give them official positions, no doubt due to their honesty and integrity;[17] at

[13] Sixtus IV, Bull, *Sacrosancta,* Nov. 20, 1473 (Wadding, *Annales Minorum,* XIV, 86-88); cf. Hilarius Parisiensis, *Liber Tertii Ordinis,* p. 122 f.

[14] "* * * statuimus quod procuratores, syndici, oblati et utriusque tertii Ordinis praedicti de Poenitentia [the Third Order of St. Dominic was also called *Ordo de Poenitentia* (S. Dominici)], nuncupatae personae praedictae iisdem privilegiis, immunitatibus, gratiis, favoribus concessionibus, facultatibus et indultis spiritualibus et temporalibus, praedictis fratrum Praedicatorum et Minorum Ordinibus ac illorum professoribus, domibus et locis, ac procuratoribus, syndicis, oblatis et commissis, seu alias quomodolibet per praedecessores nostros aut nos hactenus concessis et in posterum concedendis, * * * ac personis utriusque sexus de Poenitentia hujusmodi, nominatim concessa forent et concederentur expresse."—Bull, *Sacri Praedicatorum et Minorum,* July 26, 1479 (*Bull. Rom.,* V, 280, § 7).

[15] Bull, *Detestanda;* cf. above, footnote 8.

[16] Sept 20, 1291 (*Bull. Franc.,* IV, n. 551, p. 293 f).

[17] Cf. Callaey, *The Third Order of St. Francis,* p. 26 f.

times they were permitted to do this, especially in their care of hospitals and municipal properties; in this event the civil authorities could demand the inspection of their account books.[18]

They also had the right of exemption from interdict in regard to their spiritual exercises; Honorius III permitted them to perform their spiritual functions where divine services were allowed to be held by Apostolic Indult during the time of interdict.[19] In 1264 this privilege was also accorded to the Tertiaries of Tuscia.[20] At times it was abused, and therefore some congregations of Tertiaries were deprived of it for a time,[21] while others lost the use of it altogether.[22]

However, these local changes did not affect the general status of the penitents (Tertiaries) in this regard, for several papal decrees favored it,[23] in particular that of Sixtus IV.[24]

It was but natural that as the privileges of the Regular Orders were curtailed, especially in certain countries, so also

[18] *O. c.*, p. 28.

[19] "* * * cum igitur per Italiam tales esse nonnulli dicantur, a quibus fratres de poenitentia nuncupati, discretioni vestrae per Apostolica scripta mandamus, quatenus vos eos in ecclesiis, in quibus a Sede Apostolica est concessa generaliter tempore interdicti hujusmodi; dummodo ipsi causam Interdicti non dederint; ad divina officia, quae suppressa voce, Interdictis, et Excommunicatis exclusis, non pulsatis campanis, et clausis januis celebrantur; et Ecclesiastica Sacramenta, necnon sepulturam Ecclesiasticam admittatis."—Dec. 1, 1224 (*Bull. Franc.*, I, n. 16, p. 19 f).

[20] Urban IV, July 5, 1264 (*Bull. Franc. Epitome*, n. 1200).

[21] John XXII, March 1, 1322 (*Bull. Franc.*, V, n. 462, p. 222 f).

[22] Clement V, Nov. 14, 1306 or Nov. 13, 1307 (*o. c.*, n. 95, p. 42).

[23] Innocent IV, Aug. 31, 1357 (*o. c.*, VI, n. 726, p. 306); Boniface IX, June 24, 1403 (*o. c.*, VII, n. 465, p. 170); Martin V, Dec. 8, 1427 (*o. c.*, n. 1800, p. 692).

[24] Quoted above in footnote 14; since they were conceded all the privileges of the Friars Minor, one of which was exemption from interdict (by decree of March 29, 1222—*o. c.*, n. 10, p. 9), this privilege was also communicated to them.

were those of the Tertiaries withdrawn, particularly in regard to temporalities. In 1514 Pope Leo X confirmed all the liberties and ecclesiastical immunities granted to the Tertiaries by previous papal decrees, and which religious persons enjoyed 'quatenus sunt in usu.'[25] But two years later the same pope declared that the Tertiaries could be cited in a secular court, and that they were obliged to accept all offices which ordinarily were incumbent upon the laity. They, however, retained the right of choosing their place of burial, and of access to divine services during the time of interdict, provided they had not been the cause of the interdict, or that they had not fomented the cause of this condition in any way.[26] Thus the Tertiaries were deprived of the *privilegium fori, canonis, and immunity from civil offices;*[27] but where the contrary custom prevailed, Tertiaries were still allowed to retain the right of exemption;[28] it was definitely declared to be abolished by the same Congregation, May 13, 1727[29] and authors agree that after these decisions these privileges were no longer enjoyed by the Secular Tertiaries.[30]

The most plausible reasons that the Secular Tertiaries enjoyed these privileges are because they wore the full habit of the Franciscan Order, and also for the reason that the Rule which they followed was almost as strict as the Religious Orders of that time; hence in the wide sense they

[25] Bull, *Exponi Nobis,* Jan. 6, 1514 (Wadding, *Annales Minorum,* XV, 665 f).

[26] Bull, *Dum Intra,* Dec. 19, 1516 (*Bull. Capuc.,* VI, 224).

[27] Ferraris, *s. v. Tertiarii,* n. 22; the same tenor was expressed several times by the *S. C. of Immunity:* July 26, 1633; Nov. 22, 1633; July 19, 1635; Sept. 7, 1638; Dec. 20, 1667; May 13, 1727 (*Ibidem*); cf. Bened. XIV, *Institutiones Ecclesiasticae,* CV, LXVIII; Hilarius Parisiensis, *Liber Tertii Ordinis,* p. 136, n. 5.

[28] *S. C. of Immunity,* May 19, 1695 (Ferraris, *o. c.,* n. 23.

[29] Ferraris, *l. c.*

[30] Ferraris, *s. v. Tertiarii,* n. 59; cf. Bened. XIV, *Institutiones Ecclesiasticae,* l. c.; Hilarius Parisiensis, *Liber Tertii Ordinis,* l. c.

were considered as ecclesiastical persons, and were accorded the same privileges. But when in public they gradually assumed the scapular and cord in place of the full habit,[81] and their Rule of life was mitigated, they lived more as seculars, and hence were looked upon as such, rather than as religious and clerics: therefore the logical sequence was that their temporal exemptions were to be no more bountiful than those given to the laity in general.[82]

The privileges granted to the Tertiaries were without doubt the greatest and most munificent that have ever been accorded to any lay association by the Holy See. The solemn approval of the Third Order in 1289, and its implicit sanction through these concessions are indicative of the great esteem in which the organization, its members and its principles were held by the Roman pontiffs.

Article IV

Changes in the Third Order Secular of St. Francis.

§ 1. Adaptation of the Third Order to Changing Times.

Privileges.

A considerable number of privileges, especially temporal, have already been considered in the treatment of the question regarding the legal status of the Order and its consequent approval by the Holy See. The first change in the Rule itself is that of taking oaths, which had been forbidden

[81] Cf. Ferraris, *o. c.*, nn. 36 and 55.

[82] *Liber Joannis a Capistrano: Defensorium privilegiorum Tertii Ordinis.* The work is not accessible; the points taken from his defense are given above from Hilarius Parisiensis, *Liber Tertii Ordinis*, p. 133, n. 14; for the complete *Defensorium*, cf. *Ibidem*, p. 803-845.

under all conditions by Honorius III in 1221,[1] but which Gregory IX allowed 'to preserve peace, to maintain the faith, to clear themselves of a calumny, and to bear witness in court'.[2]

The Rule given by Nicholas IV, with its accompanying solemn approval of the Order, changed very little but rather concerned itself with a more systematic arrangement.[3] Between the time of the first Rule and that of Nicholas IV, changes had been made regarding the frequentation of the Sacraments of confession and communion: the first Rule (V, 1) prescribes confession and communion three times a year, while XIII, 3 demands monthly confession; the latter, which was obviously added at a later date, would also seem to imply more frequent communion. An Italian text of the Rule[4] demands weekly confession and daily attendance at Mass: it would not be extending the text to assert that this Rule presupposed the reception of Holy Communion more than three times yearly. Nicholas IV in his rule again changed this to three times yearly (Cap. VI).

But this did not prevent the Tertiaries from going more often if they desired: the Holy See itself favored the more frequent reception of the Sacraments when it allowed the Tertiaries access to divine services during the time of interdict. The Statutes of Innocent XI mentioned that the

[1] Bull, *Significatum est Nobis,* Dec. 6, 1221 (*Bull. Franc.*, I, n. 8, p. 8).

[2] Bull, *Detestanda,* March 30, 1228 (*o. c.*, n. 20, p. 39 f); this was added to the original Rule (*Regula Antiqua*) under V, 4.

[3] Bull, *Supra Montem,* Aug. (for the exact date cf. p. 38 above), 1289 (*Bull. Franc.*, IV, p. 94-97); the Rule is also contained in: *Seraphicae Legislationis Textus Originales,* 77-94; Antonius de Cipressa, *Regula sive Modus Vivendi Fratrum de Poenitentia S. Francisci,* p. 63-81.

Eucharist should be received for grave causes to be determined by the visitor; also on all feasts of Our Lord, the Blessed Virgin, the saints of the Order and at other times according to the discretion of the confessor.[5] The Rule of Leo XIII mentioned that it should be received monthly (II §5).

Nicholas IV made no noteworthy changes in regard to fasting. In 1527 Clement VII changed the beginning of the daily fast by placing it, not on the feast of St. Martin (as in the Rule of Nicholas IV, V), but on the first Sunday of Advent.[6] Paul III confirmed this and mitigated the fasts prescribed by Nicholas IV by abolishing the Monday abstinence, and also the fasts on all Wednesdays between the feast of All Saints and Easter; this change was originally made only for the Tertiaries of Spain, Portugal and the West Indies, but was later adopted for all Tertiaries.[7]

The Third Order has always been privileged with many indulgences and other spiritual benefits. In 1307 Clement V granted indulgences to Tertiaries for reading the Rule;[8] Boniface IX made the concession of a plenary indulgence at the hour of death.[9]

Papal munificence could not have been any greater and more favorable than that of Sixtus IV, for in 1479 he granted to the Third Order Secular of St. Francis the complete and plenary communication of all indulgences and privileges, both temporal and spiritual, which has been given in the past or were to be given in the future to the Order of Friars

[4] *A. F. H.*, XIII [1920], p. 38.

[5] Ad Cap. VI.

[6] *Orbis Seraphicus*, II, 903-911.

[7] Wadding, *Annales Minorum*, XVIII, 435-460; chap. 6, p. 467 f); cf. *Statuta Innocentiana*, Ad cap. V.

[8] *A. F. H.*, I [1908], p. 114.

[9] Nov. 22, 1402 (*Bull. Franc.*, VII, n. 435, p. 156).

Minor and the Order of Preachers, and to any of their members or places under their care; hence besides the great number of indulgences, this concession also included immunity from interdict, the privilege of celebrating Mass on a portable altar, (*altare portatile in quovis honesto loco, etiam tempore interdicti*),[10] and innumerable other benefits, both temporal and spiritual.[11] Clement VII and Paul III extended this to include the communication between the Third Order and the four mendicant Orders.[12]

Benedict XIII, due to misunderstandings which had arisen, renewed all privileges and indulgences which had previously been granted; for the sake of clarity, the text is given in full:

"Quascumque insuper litteras et gratias tam spirituales quam temporales, concessiones, indulgentias, exemptiones, indulta, privilegia, communicationes, extensiones, libertates, prearogativas, favores, peccatorum remissiones, et similia, tam in genere quam in specie, fratribus et sororibus de Poenitentia. eorumque monasteriis, domibus, conservatoriis, aut aliis quovis nomine nuncupatis habitationibus, ecclesiis etiam, oratoriis et capellis, vel immediate et directe, aut etiam per communicationem cum aliis Ordinibus et praesertim fratrum Minorum, a Romanis Pontificibus antecessoribus nostris quomodolibet concessa (quorum tenorem, ac si de verbo ad verbum his nostris litteris insereretur, haberi volumus pro expresso) harum serie approbamus et confirma-

[10] Granted to the Friars Minor Conventual and the Tertiaries by the same Pontiff in the Bull, *Regimini universalis Ecclesiae*, Aug. 31, 1474, § 4 (*Bull. Rom.*, V, 217-223); this Bull is called the *Mare Magnum* of the Franciscan Order on account of the great number of privileges it contains—cf. *o. c.*, 217; Hilarius Parisiensis, *Liber Tertii Ordinis*, p. 124.

[11] Bull, *Sacri Praedicatorum et Minorum*, July 26, 1479 (*Bull Rom.*, V, 278-283, § 7; also in *Bull. Capuc.*, VI, 199-203); this Bull is called the *Bulla Aurea* of the Franciscan and Dominican Orders for the same reasons as given in the footnote above; the text of the concession is quoted above p. 61.

[12] Ferraris, *s. v. Tertiarii*, n. 50.

mus, ac, pro potiori cautela, apostolica auctoritate singula de novo concedimus et largimur." [13]

Clement XII also added the communication of indulgences with the Brothers and Sisters of the Confraternity of the Blessed Virgin of Mt. Carmel. This was given only for the Tertiaries under the jurisdiction of the Friars Minor Capuchin,[14] and was later recalled by Benedict XIV.[15] However, due to various decrees of the Holy See which had rendered many of the indulgences and privileges doubtful,[16] Benedict XIV revoked all indulgences and privileges heretofore granted and at the same time drew up a new authentic list.[17] One hundred years later the communication of indulgences and privileges was again renewed when Pius IX revoked this Bull of Benedict XIV; this was confirmed by a decision of the Congregation of Indulgences which renewed previous communications by declaring that Tertiaries of St. Francis enjoy 'omnes et singulas indulgentias, privilegia, communicationes, . . . Tertiariis S. Francisci a glorioso Praedecessore suo Benedicto XIII concessas, tam vigore Constitutionis *Paternae Sedis,* die 10 Dec. 1725,[18] quam alterius, *Singularis devotio,* die 5 Julii 1726,[19] atque ab ipsa Sanctitate Pio IX, tum Tertiariis Franciscalibus Galliarum

[13] Benedict XIII, Bull, *Paternae Sedis Apostolicae,* Dec. 10, 1725, § 3 (*Bull Rom.,* XXII, 286); the context indicates that this had reference to the Third Order *Regular* as well as *Secular.*

[14] Bull, *Sollicitudo Pastoralis officii,* March 13, 1736 (*o. c.,* XXIV, 122 f).

[15] Bull, *Romanus Pontifex,* March 12, 1754 (*Bull. Rom. Continuatio,* I, 353 f).

[16] Cf. the decision of the *S. C. of Indulgences,* Feb. 5, 1735 (*Decreta Autheitica S. C. Indulg.,* n. 107) which is mentioned by Benedict XIV in § 2 as being given Feb. 5, 1736.

[17] Bull, *Ad Romanum Pontificem,* March 15, 1751 (*Bull. Rom. Continuatio,* III, 257-260).

[18] *Bull. Rom.,* XXII, 285-294.

[19] *O. c.,* 370-373.

per litteras Apostolicas in forma Brevis, *Supremi Apostolatus,* die 7 Julii 1848 confirmatas, tum per alias litteras, *Cum sicut nobis nuper,* die 11 Martii 1851 ad preces Rmi P. M. Generalis Ord. Conventualium S. Francisci concessas, . . . Non obstantibus Constitutione Benedicti XIV anni 1751, quae incipit *Ad Romanum Pontificem . . .*" [20]

When Leo XIII in 1883 drew up a new Rule for the Franciscan Third Order Secular, he abolished all previous indulgences and privileges, and instead granted a new list.[21] Nevertheless Pius X saw fit to grant the intercommunication of *indulgences* between the Tertiaries, and the First and Second Order.[22]

In order to gain the indulgences of the Third Order it was considered necessary to wear the full habit,[23] although after 1703, the scapular with cincture was considered as a *parvum habitum* and was allowed to be conferred as a habit by the Congregation of Bishops and Regulars;[24] this decision was later approved by the same Congregation when it declared that the habit of the Third Order meant not only the entire garment (*vestem totalem*) but also the scapular and cord.[25]

Tertiaries also enjoyed precedence over all confraternities in procession, provided they wore either the small or full

[20] Apr. 14, 1856—cf. Antonius de Cipressa, *o. c.,* p. 143 f; Hilarius Parisiensis, *o. c.,* p. 141, n. 2; *Decreta Authentica S. C. Indulg.,* n. 375.

[21] Const., *Misericors Dei Filius,* May 30, 1883 (*Fontes,* n. 588).

[22] Brief, *Sodalium e Tertio Ordine,* May 5, 1909 (*A. M.,* XVIII, 174-176).

[23] Thus Ferraris, *s. v. Tertiarii,* n. 34, in commenting on the various papal decrees giving authority to the Friars Minor to vest with the habit; cf. also Antonius de Cipressa, *o. c.,* p. 87 f; Hilarius Parisiensis, *o. c.,* p. 142.

[24] Ferraris, *l. c.;* Benedict XIII in giving jurisdiction to the Friars Minor Capuchin (Bull, *Ratio Apostolici Ministerii,* June 23, 1726—*Bull Rom.,* XXII, 368, § 2) cites this decision which states that they have jurisdiction to confer the '*habitum seu scapulare parvum cum cingulo.*'

[25] Antonius de Cipressa, *o. c.,* p. 87.

habit;[26] they were also privileged to take part in processions with the Friars Minor under the cross of the latter.[27] Precedence over all lay confraternities in procession was confirmed by the Congregation of Bishops and Regulars, Sept. 20, 1748, and by the Congregation of Rites, May 28, 1886.[28]

Franciscan Tertiaries were also permitted to use the Franciscan Breviary.[29]

Due to the great number of changes which had been made in the Rule of Nicholas IV by various papal decrees and dispensations, it was not observed in its full rigor in the nineteenth century. Therefore for the sake of uniformity, and in order to have a complete Rule which could be presented to all Franciscan Tertiaries, Leo XIII in 1883 drew up new regulations and officially confirmed them by their solemn publication in the Constitution, *Misericors Dei Filius,* May 30, 1883. This Rule is the norm by which all the Franciscan Secular Tertiaries are now guided, no matter under what jurisdiction they may be.[30]

§ 2. Tendency toward the Religious Life.

Already in the thirteenth century there was a tendency among some of the Tertiaries to unite in community life, not at first with any vows of religion, but for the particular purpose of striving after greater perfection, by being segregated from the snares of the world. The first notable example seems to have occurred in Germany, where many of the Brothers and Sisters of penance led a community life in

[26] Benedict XIII, July 22, 1728 (Antonius de Cipressa, *l. c.;* Ferraris, *l. c.*).

[27] Benedict XIII, Bull, *Paterna Sedis Apostolicae,* Dec. 10, 1725, § 9 (*Bull. Rom,* XXII, 290).

[28] *Decreta Authentica S. C. R.,* n. 3664.

[29] S. C. of Rites, Aug. 30, 1687 (Ferraris, *s. v. Officium,* Art. III, n. 56.

[30] The Constitution and the Rule may be found in the *Fontes,* n. 588; the Rule is also given below in the appendix to this dissertation.

separate houses; Pope Boniface VIII allowed them to have their own chapel.[31]

Again in many other places, communities of workingmen joined the Third Order in order to acquire a legal status and to partake in the spiritual privileges. Thus in 1289 many groups of Beghard weavers in the Netherlands adopted the Rule of the Third Order and later organized a federation of communities. In 1346 delegates from seventeen houses of the Beghards passed a resolution that none but Tertiaries be admitted to membership in their weaving organization.[32]

These did not at first take the vows of religion, but remained *Secular* Tertiaries, with the simple promise of obedience to their minister for the purposes of good government; they also remained single. It was but natural that this should have led to the religious life, and this is particularly noticeable toward the close of the fourteenth century, when the solemn vows of obedience with regular habit and cloister were added to the Rule of Nicholas IV by Boniface IX and others.[33]

The first group of Tertiary nuns was founded at Foligno in 1397. Boniface IX and Martin V allowed other convents of the Third Order to be founded, subject to the government of a Superior-General (a nun).[34]

[31] Bull, *Cupientes cultum*, July 11, 1295 (*Bull. Franc. Epitome*, n. 2027, p. 204).

[32] Callaey, *The Third Order of St. Francis*, p. 57.

[33] Wadding, *Annales Minorum*, IX, ad an. 1397, n. 31, p. 444; X, ad an. 1435, n. 18, p. 238 f; cf. *ibidem*, ad an. 1377, n. 3, p. 2.

[34] Callaey, *o. c.*, p. 58 f; Hilarius Parisiensis, *Liber Tertii Ordinis*, p. 51; Jacobili, *Vita della B. Angelina*, Bologna, 1659; *Orbis Seraphicus*, II, 837-922, particularly p. 842; Benedict XIII, Bull, *Paterna Sedis Apostolicae*, Dec. 10, 1725, § 1 (*Bull. Rom.*, XXII, 296): "* * * Ordo, pro utriusque sexus christifidelibus in ipso saeculo et in conjugio propriisque domibus manentibus a beato Francisco institutus, nonnisi quartodecimo labente saeculo in Italia praesertim ad statum religionis fuerit evectus * * *"; cf. *Etudes Franciscaines*, XXV, p. 296.

Congregations also sprang up in Belgium and the Netherlands, whose members lived a community life; Boniface IX allowed them the solemn vows of chastity and obedience and gave them authority to hold Chapters for the election of their Superiors; clerics could possess benefices with the permission of their Superiors, *'cum Regula dicti Tertii Ordinis abdicationem proprietatis non contineat.'*[85] John XXII confirmed the statutes of the Belgian Congregations and added the solemn vow of chastity;[86] he also defended these Tertiaries against the civil magistrates by declaring them to be ecclesiastical persons with the favor of all privileges and ecclesiastical immunities 'enjoyed by other Religious and ecclesiastical persons.'[87]

Other Congregations arose in the same manner in parts of France, whose members had visitors according to the Rule of Nicholas IV and lived under the immediate direction of a local Superior; John XXII counseled that these visitors should be selected from the Friars Minor; in 1447 they were given permission to hold a General Chapter by Nicholas V—they availed themselves of this privilege the following year and elected a Vicar-General.[88]

These congregations naturally spread and had a diversity of Rules, especially regarding enclosure. To remove this difference in the Rule of the various communities of men and women, and to give them the three solemn vows of poverty, chastity, and obedience with the obligation of enclosure, together with all the consequent privileges accorded to Religious, Leo X, in 1521, solemnly approved this branch of

[85] Hilarius Parisiensis, *o. c.*, p. 56; Boniface IX, Bull, *His quae divini*, Jan. 18, 1401 (Wadding, *Annales Minorum*, IX, n. 44, p. 462 f).

[86] Bull, *Personae vacantes*, Oct. 26, 1413 (*Bull. Franc.*, VII, n. 1308, p. 471-473).

[87] Bull, *Pastoralis officii cura*, March 31, 1414 (*o. c.*, *n.* 1315, p. 475 f); cf. also, *ibidem*, n. 1316.

[88] Hilarius Parisiensis, *o. c.*, p. 57.

the Third Order under the title *'Third Order Regular'*; he also gave them a uniform set of Rules.[89]

The present treatise has attempted to give only a short sketch of the development of this institution, and therefore no latitude has been given to the various branches of diocesan Sisterhoods and Congregations of men which have risen in recent years and developed from this institution.

[89] Bull, *Inter Caetera*, Jan. 20, 1521 (*Seraphicae Legislationis Textus Originales*, 287-297); its modern approval and Rule according to present Canon Law was given in the Constitution, *Rerum condicio*, of Pius XI, Oct. 4, 1927 (*A. A. S.*, XIX [1927], 361-367; *Commentarium O. F. M. Conv.*, an. XXIV, 309-315).

PART II.

PRESENT CANONICAL LEGISLATION

PART II

PRESENT CANONICAL LEGISLATION ON THE THIRD ORDER SECULAR OF ST. FRANCIS

CHAPTER VI

Definition and Purpose of the Third Order Secular of St. Francis.

ARTICLE I.

Definition.

Some idea of the elements of a Third Order Secular has already been gained from the narration of its historical as well as canonical development. The fundamental idea of all lay associations in any way approximating the subject of this treatise has always been the desire to preserve some manner of connection with a religious Order. The Church is highly desirous that lay people become members of associations which have been approved by legitimate ecclesiastical authority,[1] and divides them into Third Order Secular, confraternities and pious unions.[2]

Canon law does not give a definition of the Third Order Secular as such, but rather limits itself to a description of its members in the following manner: "Tertiarii saeculares

[1] Can. 684.

[2] Can. 700.

sunt qui in saeculo, sub moderatione alicujus Ordinis, secundum ejusdem spiritum, ad christianam perfectionem contendere nituntur, modo saeculari vitae consentaneo, secundum regulas ab Apostolica Sede pro ipsis approbatas."[3]

The Third Order Secular of St. Francis is essentially an ecclesiastical society: otherwise it could not have the approval of legitimate ecclesiastical authority.[4] It is an association in a rather wide sense of that term, for it cannot be called such because of the fact that its members constitute one body canonically grouped under one head, for this is lacking in the Franciscan Third Order; rather it is an association because Franciscan Tertiaries are joined together by the bond of one and the same Rule for all: by the bond of tending in the same spirit toward a definite end-perfect Christian charity.[5]

For the same reason, the Franciscan Third Order Secular must be called an ecclesiastical society, for it has always been approved by the Holy See; but on the other hand it cannot be called a moral person. Is the Third Order Secular *as an Order* erected by the Church, or rather merely *approved* by it? If the former is true then it possesses one of the essential requisites of a moral person; if not, then it cannot possess that juridical quality.[6] The Code itself in-

[3] Can. 702, § 1.

[4] "Nulla in Ecclesia recognoscitur associatio quae legitima auctoritate ecclesiastica erecta vel saltem approbata non fuerit." (Can. 686, § 1.)

[5] Thus Pius X, in his Apostolic Letter, *Septimo jam pleno*, Oct. 4, 1909 (*A. A. S.*, I [1909], 725-738), IX although *ratione nominis* forbids calling the Tertiaries *Leonine Union, Conventual*, or *Capuchin* for the reason that all are *Franciscan* Tertiaries, nevertheless distinguishes between these three *ratione jurisdictionis*, when he states that all have the same privileges no matter to which Franciscan Family they are subject.

[6] "Ad normam can. 100, tunc tantum fidelium associationes juridicam in Ecclesia personam acquirunt, cum a legitimo Superiore ecclesiastico formale obtinuerint erectionis decretum." (Can. 687.)

sinuates that Third Orders are merely approved when it states that Tertiaries live 'according to Rules approved by the Holy See',[7] and omits any mention of erection, while in speaking of confraternities formal erection is positively demanded.[8] Canons 687 and 703 § 1 also distinguish between approbation, aggregation, and erection. Benedict XIII, in his approval of the Franciscan Third Order Secular mentions nothing of erection, but uses the simple words, 'ab hac Romana Sede approbata."[9] Nowhere in the various papal approbations which the Third Order has received has there been any mention of *erection,* but rather only of *approval.*

Besides, according to canon 100 § 3, collegiate moral persons are to be considered as minors and therefore must act through some individual. But *ratione jurisdictionis* (and this is the basic element of this question) Tertiaries are distinct according as they are subject to the Friars Minor Leonine, Conventual, and Capuchin (also Third Order Regular) as stated above by Pius IX: in fact this juridical separation has frequently been emphasized by the Holy See; so much so that a Tertiary Sodality erected, e. g. by the Friars Minor *Capuchin,* cannot be subjected to the jurisdiction, e. g. of the Friars Minor *Conventual,* without the express consent of the former, even though they (the former) have vacated the territory wherein the Sodality was erected.[10] Canon 705 also affirms this separation of jurisdiction so that a Tertiary belonging to a Sodality e. g. under the Leonine jurisdiction, cannot at the same time belong to another Sodality e. g. under the Capuchin jurisdiction; by changing from one

[7] Can. 702, § 1.

[8] Can. 708.

[9] Bull, *Paterna Sedis Apostolicae,* Dec. 10, 1725, § 3 (*Bull. Rom.,* XXII, 287).

[10] *S. C. of Religious,* Dec. 6, 1911 (*A. A. S.,* II [1912], 143).

to the other he loses membership in the Sodality he has left: therefore he also loses his juridical rights.

Since then the bond which unites these Tertiaries who are under the various jurisdictions is fraternal, rather than juridical, it is evident that this essential quality of juridical connection and subjection is lacking in the Franciscan Third Order as a whole. The same argument may be used regarding the election of officials. Granted momentarily that the Third Order as such was legitimately erected, it would have the right to elect its officials:[11] but this election would be both illogical and impossible, for since Tertiaries under distinct jurisdictions have no juridical connections, it is incompatible with the concept of a moral person that they can unite in such an election when there is no juridical bond between them; hence the Third Order *as such* is not a moral person. The question of the *individual Sodalities* of the Third Order as moral persons will be treated later.

Tertiaries live in the world, that is, their duties as members of a family, whether as husband, wife or child, do not interfere with their obligations as members of the Third Order. This was the express purpose of Francis in founding the Order, for he realized that the religious life which a great majority of his time wished to embrace, was incompatible with the concept of family life.[12]

Again canon 702 § 1 states that the Third Order Secular is to be under the care of a religious Order; in this the wisdom of the legislator can be seen, for immediately the same canon adds that Tertiaries are to live according to the spirit of this same religious Order. Therefore Tertiaries live in the world, but at the same time they should live up to the ideals of the Franciscan religious in so far as their

[11] Can. 697, § 1.

[12] Cf. above Chap. V, Article I on the foundation of the Third Order.

state of life permits. In glancing over the Rules of the Third Order Secular of St. Francis, a great similarity can readily be noticed between the ideals of the Franciscan religious and the Franciscan Tertiaries, especially concerning poverty, simplicity of life and the practice of Christian charity.

In order to understand more clearly the notion of the Third Order Secular of St. Francis, it might be well to compare it with other associations:

A) Although both bear the name *'Order'*, yet there is a great difference between the Third Order Regular and Secular, for the former, although an offshoot of the latter, live in community life with the vows of religion,[13] while the members of the latter live in the world with their families. The same distinction may be drawn between the three Families of the First Order (Friars Minor Leonine, Conventual and Capuchin), and the Third Order Secular. A comparison of canons 487 and 488, 2o, which speak of the religious state and its members with solemn vows, with canon 702 § 1 brings out this difference more clearly. But even with this great dissimilarity, the Third Order Secular of St. Francis always was and remains a true Order: Benedict XIII especially remonstrated against those who would reduce it to a mere confraternity, when he declared it to be a 'true and proper order, composed of seculars . . . and altogether distinct from any confraternity, for it possesses a Rule approved by the Holy See, with a novitiate, habit and profession, of a specific form, even as Regulars.'[14]

[13] Cf. above, Chapter V, Art. IV, § 2.

[14] "* * * nos eumdem sanctum, meritorium et christianae perfectioni conformem, necnon verum et proprium ordinem, unum in toto orbe ex saecularibus aliisque collegialiter viventibus et regularibus promiscue compositum, [these latter words have reference to the Third Order Regular, for Benedict XIII is speaking of both in this Bull] et a confraternitate quacumque ex comprehensis in Bulla recolendae

The same declaration was made by Leo XIII in an audience granted to the Ministers-General of the First Order and the Third Order Regular,[15] and by Benedict XV who expressly stated that 'Francis founded a true Order of Tertiaries.'[16] Consequently there is a great similarity between the Franciscan Religious Orders and the Third Order Regular, for both are true Orders with novitiate, habit and profession, and although the Third Order Secular of St. Francis 'is not bound as the other two [the First Order and the Third Order Regular] by the vows of religion, it is the same as regards simplicity of life and the practice of penance."[17]

Then again both live according to Rules approved by the Holy See, and through these aspire to perfection; the Franciscan Religious as well as the Tertiaries are bound by the ties of brotherly love—the former by their common life, the latter by their mutual help toward one another in health, in sickness and in death.[18]

B) The Third Order Secular of St. Francis differs from other associations of the laity: Benedict XIII and Leo XIII as noted above have expressly discriminated between the Franciscan Third Order Secular and other lay associations.

memoriae Clementis Papae VIII omninode distinctum, utpote qui sub propria regula ab hac Romana Sede approbata, cum novitiatu, professione et habitu, sub certis modo et forma, prout caeteri Ordines tum regulares tum militares et alii hujusmodi consueverunt, dispositus reperitur, fuisse semper et esse decernimus et declaramus."—Bull, *Paterna Sedis Apostolicae,* Dec. 10, 1725, § 4 (*Bull. Rom.,* XXII, 285-294).

[15] July 7, 1883: "Aliqui existimarunt, post recentem Constitutionem *Misericors Dei Filius,* Tertium Ordinem ad simplicem Confraternitatem et Sodalitium esse revocatum. [Talis non est nostra mens, sed uti declaravimus [in the Constitution, *Misericors Dei Filius,* May 30, 1883—*Fontes,* n. 588], ejusdem instituti natura ac essentia perseverant, et non simplex congregatio, sed verus Ordo remanet." (*A. M.,* II, 111.)

[16] Const. *Sacra propediem,* Jan. 6, 1921 (*A. A. S.,* XIII [1921], 34).

[17] *Ibidem.*

[18] Cf. Rule of Leo XIII, II, §§ 9, 13-14.

Although even the Holy See at times uses the words 'fraternity', 'confraternity' and 'sodality' to designate the Third Order Secular, this term is not used in the canonical sense, but rather in a popular sense to denote that Franciscan Tertiaries are joined into a fraternity by the common bond of their Rule; in this same sense even the Regular Orders are called fraternities: thus the words 'frater' and 'fratres' are used to designate the members of a Regular Religious Order.

The Franciscan Third Order differs from other associations of the laity by reason of its approbation: it has always been approved by the Holy See itself, while the ordinary of the place may approve other associations.[19] The same distinction can be drawn regarding the approbation of their respective Rules and Statutes according to canons 689 and 702 § 1. There is also a great contrast *ratione jurisdictionis*: the Third Order is under the jurisdiction of the Friars Minor, *seclusis locorum ordinariis*,[20] while other associations, unless they have a privilege such as the Franciscan Third Order Secular enjoys, are under the jurisdiction of the ordinary of the place.[21]

Membership in this institution is a state of life which in itself tends to perfection: other associations as a rule have some *particular* virtue or end in view.[22]

The Third Order Secular also differs from other associations of the laity by reason of its membership: thus religious with either temporary or perpetual vows are forbidden

[19] Can. 686, § 2.

[20] Benedict XIII, Bull, *Paterna Sedis Apostolicae,* Dec. 10, 1725—cf. above pp. 42-45.

[21] Can. 690, § 1.

[22] Compare canon 702 with canon 707. "Tertius Ordo est multo plus quam quaedam confraternitas; est enim status vitae tendens vi status istius ad perfectionem christianam." (Prümmer, *Manuale Juris Canonici,* Q. 270.)

to become members of this association,[33] while there seems to be nothing in canon law forbidding religious as such from becoming members of confraternities and pious unions;[34] neither are Tertiaries allowed to belong to two different Third Orders at the same time,[35] although such an exclusion is not made by the Code in regard to other lay associations.

Secular Tertiaries are not ecclesiastical persons in the canonical sense of that term;[36] nevertheless in a wide sense they may be called such: 1) Because they are connected with a religious Order which has the approbation of the Holy See; 2) for the reason that this same Holy See has also approved the Order of Tertiaries; 3) because they observe a Rule which in many ways partakes of the religious state.

Tertiaries also differ vastly from Cord-bearers (*Confraternitas Chordigerorum*) in:

1) Institution—The Third Order Secular was founded by St. Francis; the Confraternity of Cord-bearers by Sixtus V.

2) Nature—the one is an Order; the other a simple confraternity.

3) Rules—the Rules of the Third Order Secular are approved by the Holy See; those of the Cord-bearers by the ordinary of the place.

4) Habit—Tertiaries wear a cord and habit, or a scapular in place of the latter; Cord-bearers, as the name implies, wear only a cord.[37]

[33] Can. 704, §1.

[34] Cf. canons 707-726.

[35] Can. 705.

[36] Formerly they had all the privileges of ecclesiastical persons—cf. above Chap. V, Art. III.

[37] Mocchegiani, *Collectio Indulgentiarum*, n. 1532; Mocchegiani, *Jurisprudentia Ecclesiastica*, II, n. 679.

ARTICLE II

Purpose of the Third Order Secular of St. Francis.

The purpose of the Third Order Secular is very concisely summarized in canon 702 which states that Tertiaries live in the world under the care of the [Franciscan] Order and according to its spirit, in conformity with their lives as laity. The primary end of the Third Order was the same in the beginning as it is now: to offer to its members a Rule of life which is more conducive to christian perfection than the means ordinary christians have at their disposal. The Tertiaries, besides those norms which are common to the laity in general, have special Rules and precepts which tend to a more christian perfection, although they do not bind under sin.[1]

An understanding of the purpose of the Franciscan Third Order could best be arrived at by determining the primary object of its foundation by St. Francis, by ascertaining the incentive which the laity of his time had in becoming members of such an organization, for as Leo XIII and other pontiffs have stated, the nature of the Third Order remains the same as it was in the beginning.[2] Therefore looking into the primary object which induced the foundation of the Franciscan Third Order Secular, history relates that the

[1] Thus the first Rule of the Order: "In supradictis omnibus [Regulis] nemo obligatur ad culpam, sed ad poenam * * *" (XII, 7); "In his legibus si qui forte quid deliquerint, hoc se nomine culpam suscepturos nullam sciant * * *" (*Rule of Leo XIII*, III, § 5).

[2] Leo XIII, Const. *Misericors Dei Filius*, May 30, 1883 (*Fontes*, n. 588); the words of the same pontiff in an audience granted to the Ministers-General of the First Order and the Third Order Regular, July 7, 1883: "* * * ejusdem natura ac essentia perseverant, * * *" (A. M., II, 111); Benedict XIII, Bull, *Paterna Sedis Apostolicae*, Dec. 10, 1725, § 4 (*Bull. Rom.*, XXII, 285-294).

Saint wished to give the laity, upon their own plea, a Rule of life which was near to the evangelical precepts, and closely approximated the religious life, and still did not destroy family life, and their necessary environment in, and their contact with the world as seculars and laity.[3] This principle is very clearly embodied in the definition of Tertiaries as contained in canon 702 § 1, as well as in recent papal pronouncements. Thus Leo XIII in describing the foundation of the Third Order, states that 'with a wonderful simplicity and perseverance, St. Francis began to hold up to a decadent world, in word and in deed, the true ideal of christian perfection, . . . leading it back from a long aberration to the imitation of Christ.'[4]

Again in the solemn approval of the mitigated Rule of the Third Order of St. Francis, the same pontiff declares that the 'Third Order of St. Francis is based entirely on the observance of the precepts of Jesus Christ. The Holy Founder had no other object in view than that the Order should be a kind of training school for a more intensive practice of the christian Rule of life.'[5] Franciscan Tertiaries should especially tend to christian perfection by the simplicity of their lives,[6] and especially are they to practice Christian charity toward their brethren both in life[7] and in death.[8]

[3] Cf. above chap. V, Art. I; Leo XIII, Encyclical, *Auspicato,* Sept. 17, 1882 (*A. S. S.,* XV, 149 f).

[4] Encyclical, *Auspicato* (*o. c.,* 147).

[5] Const., *Misericors Dei Filius,* May 30, 1883 (*Fontes,* n. 588).

[6] *Rule of Leo XIII,* II, § 1: "Sodales Tertii Ordinis in omni cultu habituque, sumptuosiore elegentia posthabita, teneant eam, quae singulos deceat, mediocritatis regulam."

[7] *O. c.,* II, § 9: "Caritatem benevolam et inter se et ad alienos sedulo tueantur."

[8] *O. c.,* II, § 14: "Ad exsequias sodalis demortui sodales municipes hospitesve conveniant, simulque * * * preces * * * ad coeleste demortui

Especially should they take care that books of a tainted character are not read, and in order to hold to the traditions of their faith, the Sacrifice of the Mass should be attended frequently in their parish church; as a means of preserving the faith in themselves and in others, they should not hesitate to assist in the instruction of the young regarding christian doctrine. There is no doubt that the greatest means of acquiring this christian sanctity is through its practical application: by the avoidance of discordance, by the care of the sick through alms; in one word: works of mercy cannot be encouraged too strenuously.[9] And if the Tertiaries are equipped to aid the needy in their manifold wants, they shall be no less charitable in assisting those who are in need of those things which are above the material: this especially by means of a good example, so that 'our Franciscan Tertiaries by purity of faith, by innocence of life, and by cheerful zeal, shall diffuse far and wide the good odor of Christ, and be to the brethren that have gone astray both a reminder and an invitation to come to a sense of their duties. This the Church asks, this she expects of them.'[10]

Pius X especially concerned himself with explicitly defining the purpose and scope of the Third Order Secular of St. Francis. There is no doubt that in many localities the true purpose of this Order: the acquirement of christian perfec-

solatium adhibeant. Item sacerdotes inter rem divinam, laici, si poterunt, sumpta Eucharistia, pacem fratri defuncto sempiternam pii volentes adprecentur."

[9] Pius X, Const., *Tertium Franciscalium Ordinem*, Sept. 8, 1912 (*A. A. S.*, IV [1912], 584).

[10] Benedict XV, Const., *Sacra propediem*, Jan. 6, 1921 (*A. A. S.*, XIII [1921], 39 f).

tion by adhering as closely as possible to the evangelical precepts, by assistance to others in both material and spiritual matters, had been greatly distorted; hence 'we shall not conceal a fear produced in Us for some time by certain symptoms that an unwise zeal for modernity, on the plea of being of greater service to society, is insinuating itself in some places in the Order of Tertiaries, and gradually turning it aside from its original scope as conceived by the most holy Francis.'

The pontiff goes on to explain that the scope of the Third Order today is the same as in the time of its founder, and as has been handed down through the various Apostolic Constitutions.

'Therefore from what has been said, it is Our opinion that the institute of the Third Order consists in this: that its members make use of the evangelical precepts in their daily lives, and hold up to others this example of a christian life. Consequently Third Order Sodalities as such (qua talia) should by no means be concerned with civil and merely economical dealings; if they do this they therefore realize that they are deviating from the purpose of this institute and are operating against our will.'[11]

On the contrary it is highly praiseworthy that Tertiaries as individuals, become members of Catholic societies which have a peculiar end in view; neither are they prohibited from doing social work (actione sociali) such as has been approved by the Holy See; but the Third Order as such, is especially prohibited from invading the realms of society or to make such a purpose its own.[12]

From the preceding part of his Constitution it is evident

[11] Pius X, Const., *Tertium Franciscalium Ordinem*, Sept. 8, *1912* (*A. A. S.*, IV [1912], 582-585).

[12] *Ibidem.*

that Pius X had in mind the works of mercy, and the instruction of the ignorant and the young in christian doctrine when he referred to 'social work'. This is also evident from a decree of the Sacred Consistorial Congregation, which under the heading 'De Operibus piis et socialibus', describes social work as the provision for the moral and religious end of the faithful, as well as the provision for their temporal needs by works of mercy.[13] But if a Tertiary should found a new society for either a pious or charitable purpose, even though the Franciscan Superiors may be called the authors of it in a wide sense, it is nevertheless entirely under the jurisdiction of the bishop.[14]

The reason for this is apparent, for the Third Order Secular has not an individual purpose in view such as most confraternities and pious associations; it has rather a more general and higher purpose of christian perfection, which may indeed be, and is acquired through works of charity and other pious causes, but at the same time it is forbidden that any of these works be made the principal end and purpose of the Third Order.

Neither can it be objected that the oft-quoted words of Leo XIII—'*my social reform is the Third Order*'—are opposed to those of Pius X who prohibits the Third Order as such from engaging itself too freely in economic and social affairs. A perusal of all the pronouncements of Leo XIII on the Third Order will cause such an objection to vanish, for he stresses the spiritual and religious side of the Third Order just as strenuously, and perhaps even more so than the later pontiff.[15] By social reform Leo XIII does not mean

[13] Dec. 31, 1909, n. 143 (*A. A. S.*, II [1910], 33).

[14] Pius X, Const. *Tertium Franciscalium Ordinem, l. c.*

[15] Cf. passim the collection of the various decrees of Leo XIII on the Third Order—Fleming, *Leonis XIII Acta ad III Ordinem Spectantia.*

to insinuate that the Tertiaries are to engage *as an Order* in those activities which Pius X prohibits them to embrace in the same manner, but he does state, and the conclusion is logical, that if the Rule and the precepts of the Third Order are followed everywhere, the social aspect of the world will be changed for the better, that the lives of the people will be reformed, because of the fact that the observance of these rules necessarily is conducive toward christian charity and perfection.

Thus Leo XIII, speaking of the early times of the Third Order states that it 'formed a solid bulwark of public safety. Keeping in view the virtues and precepts of their founder, the members did their utmost to resuscitate in society the glorious fruits of christian morality. The fact is, by their influence and example, they often tore down or modified feuds; they snatched weapons from the hands of infuriated partisans; they removed the source of strife and contention; they brought relief to the needy and desolate; they chastised luxury, that ravener of fortunes and pander to vices. Domestic peace and public tranquility, integrity of life and kindliness, the right use and management of property—the best foundations of civilization and security—spring from the Third Order as from their root, and it is to Francis that Europe is largely indebted for the preservation of these blessings.' [16]

After describing the distressing conditions of society, the pontiff continues that 'no small hope of relief could be placed in the rule of Francis, were it restored to its former importance. With it would flourish faith and piety and all that is glorious in Christianity; the lawless craving for earth's perishable goods would be broken and, what is frequently regarded as the greatest and most hateful of bur-

[16] Encyclical, Auspicato, Sept. 17, 1882 (*A. S. S.*, XV, 150).

dens, people would no longer dread to put the bridle of virtue on their passions. . . . Furthermore, once men are thoroughly imbued with the Christian religion, they feel the conviction that it is a matter of conscience to obey lawfully constituted authority, and that no one may be molested in any of his rights.' "[17]

Innumerable other examples could be given to prove that the one purpose of the Third Order as described by recent pontiffs is that of the acquirement of christian perfection by its members, and through their consequent good example, the reform of others in like manner. Consequently the basic purpose of the Third Order as well as the other Franciscan institutions is the same today as it was in the time of St. Francis, and as has been more recently expressed by pontiffs in their pronouncements on the Third Order: "The entire Franciscan Institute is based on the observance of the precepts of Jesus Christ,"[18] which observance, as Francis has inculcated it, cannot fail to assist in uprooting some of the modern errors of Socialism and Naturalism.[19]

It might be added here that the high purpose and deep influence of the Third Order Secular of St. Francis has recently become so pronounced that it has not failed to attract attention even in Non-Catholic circles, with the result that such an institute has been founded in Protestant Churches.[20]

[17] *O. c.*, 151 f.

[18] Leo XIII, Const., *Misericors Dei Filius*, May 30, 1883 (*Fontes*, n. 588); Pius X, Const., *Tertium Franciscalium Ordinem, o. c.*, 582 f.

[19] Leo XIII, Encyclical, *Auspicato, l. c.*

[20] Cf. "Der III Orden in Protestantischer Aufmachung", *St. Franziskus*, July, 1927, nn. 1-2, pp. 13-18, where a summary of the Rules of the Third Order as embodied in Protestant sects is given.

CHAPTER VII

General Jurisdiction Over the Third Order Secular of St. Francis.

Article I.

The Roman Pontiff.

The divine institution of the Church as well as the very nature of law and order demands that at the head of all its members there should be a supreme rule subject to no one.[1] Since the Third Order Secular of St. Francis is a legitimately approved and recognized society in the Church, it follows that it has as its head the Roman Pontiff, not only by reason of the fact that its members are in communion with the Holy See, but also because it is an association with Apostolic approbation. But besides the common ties by which all ecclesiastical bodies are subject to the Pope, there are special bonds which unite the Third Order Secular of Francis under the jurisdiction of the Holy Father.

In the first place he reserves to himself the approval of the Rules of the Third Order Secular.[2] This is not a recent innovation for the Roman Pontiffs, from the very beginning of the Franciscan Third Order, have approved its Rules, made statutes accommodating the lives of the Tertiaries to the trend of the times, and have heartily voiced their ap-

[1] Can. 218.

[2] "Tertiarii saeculares * * * in saeculo * * * nituntur * * * secundum regulas *ab Apostolica Sede pro ipsis approbatas.*" (Can. 702, § 1.)

proval of the institute as a means of saving souls. Thus Honorius III and Gregory IX gave implicit approbation to the Order when they conceded many privileges to the Tertiaries and recommended them (the Tertiaries) to the bishops of Italy;[3] it received its solemn approbation and uniform Rule at the hands of Nicholas IV in 1289,[4] from which time down to the present those who have occupied the See of Peter have been most profuse in their favorable pronouncements on the Order. No religious institute is allowed to found a Third Order Secular, although such a privilege has been granted to some in the past,[5] which is precisely the case of the Franciscan Third Order Secular due to its solemn approval and recommendation to the jurisdiction of the Friars Minor, among the noteworthy of which is the Bull, *Paterna Sedis Apostolicae,* Dec. 10, 1725.[6] Hence the foundation of a Third Order Secular may be termed one of the *'causae majores'* reserved to the Roman Pontiff.[7]

The more recent manifestation of papal interest in this Order was shown by Leo XIII when he solemnly approved the institute and issued a new Rule for its members through its publication in the Constitution, *Misericors Dei Filius,* May 30, 1883.[8] The great number of privileges and indulgences which the Order has always received at the hands of the Holy See could also be adduced as a further mark of

[3] Honorius III, Bull, *Significatum est nobis,* Dec. 16, 1221 (*Bull. Francs.,* I, n. 8, p. 9); Gregory IX, Bulls, *Nimis patenter,* June 25, 1227 (*o. c.,* n. 7, p. 30 f), and *Detestanda,* March 30, 1228 (*o. c.,* n. 20, p. 39 f).

[4] Bull, *Supra montem* (*o. c.,* IV, pp. 94-97).

[5] Can. 703, § 1.

[6] *Bull. Rom.,* XXII, 285-294.

[7] Can. 220.

[8] *Fontes,* n. 588.

interest from the occupants of the See of Peter.[9]

All Tertiaries must manifest their obedience to the Holy See when in their profession they promise to obey the Rules of the Third Order as approved by Leo XIII and Nicholas IV.[10]

All the recent declarations of the Popes regarding their solicitude for the spread of the Third Order as a world power for good are always expressive of the fidelity of St. Francis toward the Holy See, and exhort his followers to imitate his example.[11] Since devotion to the Holy See is one of the chief Franciscan characteristics, Pius X especially exhorts Tertiaries to pledge their loyalty and fidelity at conventions of the Third Order.[12]

The affairs of Tertiaries are generally not treated by the Roman Pontiff himself, but are reserved by him to the *'Congregatio negotiis religiosorum sodalium praeposita'*, which treats exclusively of the government, discipline, temporal goods and privileges of the Third Order Secular.[13] However, this Congregation does not handle the affairs of Tertiaries as individuals, but rather as members of a society which they

[9] Cf. passim above chap. V, Art. III-IV.

[10] *Ceremonial of the Third Order*, Art. III.

[11] E. g. Leo XIII, Encyclical, *Auspicato*, Sept. 17, 1882 (*A. S. S.*, XV, 145-153); Pius X, Brief, *Sodalium e Tertio Ordine*, May 5, 1909 (*A. M.*, II, 174-176); Pius X, Const., *Tertium Franciscalium Ordinem*, Sept. 7, 1912 (*A. A. S.*, IV [1912], 582-586); Benedict XV, Const., *Sacra propediem*, Jan. 6, 1921 (*A. A. S.*, XIII [1921], 33-41); Pius XI, Const., *Rite expiatis*, Apr. 30, 1926 (*A. A. S.*, XVIII [1926], 153-175).

[12] Const., *Tertium Franciscalium Ordinem*, *o. c.*, n. X: "Cum Franciscalis Ordo id habet velut proprium ac singulare ut Jesu Christi Vicario arctissime adhaereat, Tertiarii suae in Romanum Pontificem ac secundo in Ordinis generales Ministros studiosae observantiae significationem, coetum ineuntes, solemniter edere ne omitant."

[13] Can. 251, § 1; Pius X, Const., *Sapienti Consilio*, Jan. 29, 1908, I, 5°, 1 (*A. A. S.*, I [1909], 9-19).

represent, namely in those things which concern the government, discipline, temporal goods and privileges of the Third Order Secular as an Order.[14]

ARTICLE II

General Jurisdiction of the Friars Minor and the Third Order Regular over the Third Order Secular of St. Francis

In a previous article the relations between the Friars Minor as well as the Third Order Regular, and the secular Franciscan Tertiaries was dwelt on with some detail.[1] The present article shall deal with their canonical authority over the Tertiaries. From the time of the foundation of the Third Order till its definite and solemn approbation by Nicholas IV in 1289, this jurisdiction went through various stages whereupon this pontiff in the Bull, *Supra Montem,* (1289) counseled (consulimus) that the first Order rule the Third.[2]

The most complete and exclusive canonical subjection of the Secular Tertiaries to the jurisdiction of the Friars Minor occurred at the hands of Benedict XIII through the Bull, *Paterna Sedis Apostolicae,* Dec. 10, 1725.[3] In this Bull he confirms and approves all former Apostolic pronouncements through which any authority, superiority and preeminence had been granted to the Minister-General and secondary Superiors of the Friars Minor over the Ter-

[14] Cf. Chelodi, *Jus de Personis,* n. 166; Cocchi, *Commentarium,* III, n. 188.

[1] Cf. Chap. 5, Art. II.

[2] *Bull. Rom.,* IV, 94, chap. 16: "Quia vero praesens vivendi forma institutionem a b. Francisco praelibato suscepit, consulimus, ut visitatores de fratrum Minorum ordine assumantur, * * *".

[3] *Bull. Rom.,* XXII, 285-294.

tiaries (§6). Even as the members of the First Order as well as the Second (Poor Clares) recognize Francis as their founder, so also all Tertiaries must recognize the Minister-General and his secondary Superiors, i. e. the provincials and guardians, as their superiors, whom they are obliged to obey in all things pertaining to the Order. As a penalty for disobedience, these same Superiors may eject them from the Third Order with the result that they shall be deprived of all indulgences and privileges.[4]

After this clear enunciation of the general jurisdiction of the Friars Minor, the pontiff descends to particulars by giving the Minister-General and secondary Superiors authority to erect Tertiary congregations (Sodalities according to the present canonical terminology—can. 702 §2) everywhere 'per patentes Litteras'; these they shall guide with full authority to change anything in the statutes which is not opposed to the Rule and sacred canons.[5] The Min-

[4] "Mandamus propterea universis et singulis hujusmodi instituti professoribus, per universum mundum existentibus, ac * * * in saeculo sub proprio tectu vel in conjugio ipso * * * degentibus, ut, sicut cum primo et secundo Ordine, Minorum scilicet et Clarissarum, unum et eumdem institutorem, auctorem et patriarcham habent, ita unum et eumdem ipsiusmet fundatoris legitimum successorem veluti patrem et caput totius seraphici gregis, atque trium Ordinum beati Francisci primarium generalem honorent, observent et recognoscant, ejusque secundarios delegatos, sive provinciales, sive guardianos, aut etiam commissarios visitatores, tamquam suos legitimos et veros superiores venerentur, ita ut ipsorum judicio in dubiis et controversiis circa regulam et statuta se conforment, atque in iis omnibus, quae concernunt Ordinem ipsum, nec regulae sunt contraria, illis pareant et obediant: quod si secus fecerint, ab iisdem cassari atque habitu spoliari possint, immo nullis proinde Tertiariorum gratiis et privilegiis gaudere decernimus et jubemus." (§ 7.)

[5] " * * * quibus propterea plenum jus ac libere auctoritatem ea innovandi, immutandi, augendi aut imminuendi, ac alia de caetero statuendi, quae bonum dicti gregis regimen concernere possunt, dummodo tamen regulae praefatae sacrique canonibus non adversentur, * * * perpetuis futuris temporibis facultatem facimus atque largimur." (§ 8.)

ister-General through his secondary Superiors can receive into the Third Order to the exclusion of all others; in the same manner they have authority to instruct in the Rule, administer the Sacraments, and preside at all elections and functions of the Sodalities. (§8)

But even this is not the full extent of the jurisdiction of the Friars Minor, for he enjoins them to perform the office of visitation by instructing in the Rule, reforming and correcting the Tertiaries, even to expulsion from the Order; this authority of visitation also extends to vigilance over Tertiary funds; but the most important canonical point of this Bull is that the ordinary of the place is positively excluded from any of this jurisdiction.[6]

This Bull, although given in favor of the Friars Minor *Observant*, has equal force for the other Franciscan Families, due to its extension by the same pontiff to the Friars Minor Capuchin,[7] Conventual[8] and Third Order Regular;[9] the same pontiff again confirmed this extension to the Friars Minor Conventual and Capuchin in 1728.[10]

This equality of jurisdiction has always been maintained down to the present time by the Holy See. Thus Clement XII reaffirms the jurisdiction of the Friars Minor Capuchin after a dispute,[11] and at the same instigation the Congregation of Bishops and Regulars Sept. 11, 1740 declared that 'all legitimate sons of St. Francis have authority over the Secular Tertiaries as was given by Benedict XIII and

[6] "privative quoad alios quoscumque"; "seclusis locorum ordinariis et aliis quibuscumque personis cujusve status." (§ 8.)

[7] Bull, *Ratio Apostolici Ministerii*, June 23, 1726 (*Bull. Rom.*, XXII, 367-370).

[8] Bull, *Singularis Devotio*, July 5, 1726 (*o. c.*, 370-375).

[9] Bull, *Exponi nobis*, Sept. 30, 1729 (*o. c.*, 856-858).

[10] Bull, *Dilecti Filii*, June 21, 1728 (*Ferraris, s. v. Tertiarii*, n. 29).

[11] Bull, *Apostolicae Servitutis*, July 23, 1735 (*Bull. Rom.*, XXIV, 61 f).

Clement XII';[12] this decision was implicitly approved when Benedict XIV, treating of the same question, embodied it in the Constitution, *Laudabile.*[13] The *Rule of Leo XIII* demands that the visitors shall be chosen from the First Order or the Third Order Regular.[14] In an audience granted to the four Ministers-General of the First Order and the Third Order Regular, Leo XIII placed upon them through their priests, the obligation of spreading the Third Order Secular.[15]

Pius X in his Brief, *Spetimo jam pleno,* Oct. 4, 1909,[16] not only states the jurisdiction of the Friars Minor over the secular Tertiaries, but insists on the equality of this jurisdiction, whether it be of the Friars Minor Leonine,[17] Conventual or Capuchin, so that the Tertiaries cannot call themselves Leonine, Conventual or Capuchin, but all are rather Franciscan Tertiaries.[18] The omission of any men-

[12] *Bull. Rom.,* Continuatio, I, 548 f.

[13] Aug. 2, 1745 (*o. c.,* 547-550).

[14] III, §3.

[15] July 7, 1883 (*A. M.,* II, 111; Fleming, *Leonis XIII Acta ad III Ordinem Spectantia,* p. 36).

[16] *A. A. S.,* I [1909], 725-739.

[17] That is, those Franciscans under the various names of '*Observantes, Reformati, Excalceati, Alcanterini, or Recollecti* whom Leo XIII declared to be under one government by the Constitution, *Felicitate Quaedam,* Oct. 4, 1897 (*A. S. S.,* XXX, 225-233).

[18] To prove these assertions the following points are taken verbatim from the Brief, *Septimo jam pleno,* of Pius X (cited above footnote 16):

IV. "Nomine Capuccinus, Conventualis, Unionis Leonianae Franciscales discriminant non id notando, quod ad rationem ipsam et naturam Fratris Minoris pertinet: hoc enim in Regula Seraphica consistit quae apud omnes Franciscales Ordinis primi una atque eadem est: verum eas designando res quae in hoc genere accidunt naturae; et hae sunt Constitutiones, quae unaquaeque familia proprias et peculiares in observanda, ex Apostolicae Sedis praescripto, sequitur.

VI. Trium familiarum Franciscalium Ministri Generales omnes sunt atque habendi sunt et dignitate er potestate pares, ut Vicarii atque

tion of the Third Order Regular by Pius X by no means excludes them from this jurisdiction, for this Brief treats *ex professo* of the First Order only. The same pontiff reaffirms the jurisdiction of the Friars Minor when he counsels that the Third Order Secular should be instituted in secular churches through legitimate delegation by the Franciscan Superiors, 'salvo semper jure et officio praelatorum Ordinis Primi."[19] The same argument may be used here regarding the omission of the Third Order Regular, for this epistle was addressed to the First Order.

Having treated of the jurisdiction of the Friars Minor over the Secular Franciscan Tertiaries,[20] the question may be asked: what kind of jurisdiction do they enjoy? The Friars Minor possess *ordinary* jurisdiction over the Tertiaries in *spiritual* matters. This spiritual authority is apparent from the very nature of the institution of the Third Order whose members primarily tend toward Christian perfection. The first authority which was accorded to the Friars Minor was of a *spiritual* nature. Subsequent legislation up to the time of Benedict XIII always concedes

adeo veri successores sancti Francisci, nempe pro sua quisque familia, atque etiam pro sodalibus Secundi et Tertii Ordinis, quotquot suae habent vel jurisdictioni subjectos vel familiae aggregatos: iidem praedecessorum suorum perpetuam seriem ab ipso Patre Seraphico omnes jure ducunt.

IX. Ministro Generales triplicis Minorum familiae pari sunt potestate in Orinem Tertium. Tertiarii propterea qui Ministro Generali unius familiae parent, privilegiis indulgentiisque fruuntur, ac qui duobus aliis subjecti sunt. Nec licebit qui Tertio Ordini adscripti sunt eos Tertiarios vel ab Unione Leoniana, vel Conventuales, vel Capuccinos, appelare, sed Tertiarios S. Francisci seu Franciscales, sine alio apposito dici oportebit.

[19] Epistle, *Tertium Franciscalium Ordinem*, Sept. 7, 1912 (*A. A. S.*, IV [1912], 585).

[20] For the purposes of this treatise, from now on the term *Friars Minor* shall be considered as comprising also the Third Order Regular unless the context denotes otherwise.

jurisdiction which is of a spiritual character, when the pontiffs enjoin the Franciscan Superiors to vest with the habit, instruct in the Rule, correct delinquencies, and generally perform the office of visitation and correction.[21]

Benedict XIII in his Bull, *Paterna Sedis Apostolicae,* Dec. 10, 1725 (given above), reaffirms this when he enjoins the Friars Minor to erect Tertiary congregations, instruct in the Rule, invest with the habit, correct infractions of the Rule and demand obedience of the Tertiaries with the penal sanction of ejection from the Order.[22] Other pontiffs have also stated the jurisdiction of the Friars Minor to be a spiritual one.[23]

Other numerous examples could be given, but suffice it to quote Leo XIII, the author of the present Rule of the Tertiaries, wherein the jurisdiction of the Friars Minor is entirely a spiritual one, embracing also the authority of mitigating the Rule in individual cases. The duties of the Director, or Moderator, as contained in the Ceremonial of the Third Order also possess merely a spiritual quality.

Conclusion: the Friars Minor enjoy ordinary spiritual jurisdiction over Tertiaries as *Tertiaries,* as also regarding the erection of Tertiary Sodalities. It is apparent that a distinction between spiritual and temporal jurisdiction must be made, for if the Friars Minor possessed both, they could also concern themselves with the temporal goods of

[21] Cf. above chap. V, Art. II.

[22] "Tertii Ordinis congregationes saeculares * * * erigere"; "utriusque sexus christifideles * * * recipere; " (§ 8) "itaut ipsorum judicio in dubiis et controversiis circa regulam et statuta se conforment, atque in iis omnibus, quae concernunt Ordinem ipsum, nec regulae sunt contraria, illis pareant et obediant". (§ 7) "visitare ac instruere, et paterne corrigere ac reformare, tam in capite quam in membris, ad cassationem usque mantelli et habitus." (§ 8.)

[23] Cf. the various Apostolic Constitutions quoted throughout this present chapter.

Third Order Sodalities. That this jurisdiction is spiritual and *spiritual alone* will be treated subsequently in the question regarding the administration of Tertiary properties. The particular and specific application of this ordinary spiritual jurisdiction which accrues to the Friars Minor will be given throughout this treatise.

CHAPTER VIII

The Particular Application of the Ordinary Spiritual Jurisdiction of the Friars Minor

Article i

The Enactment of Statutes

Jurisdiction over the Third Order Secular also implies the authority of enacting statutes by which the Sodalities of Tertiaries may the better be ruled according to local conditions. Thus Clement VII, in subjecting the Tertiaries of Spain to the Third Order Regular, at the same time affirmed that they could 'enact any statutes * * * and constitutions * * * not contrary to the sacred canons, and which tend to the stricter observance of the Order of Penance [Third Order].'[1] Statutes were then drawn up for two classes of Tertiaries: those living a community life, and for Secular Tertiaries. Paul III approved these for the Tertiaries of Spain, Portugal and India.[2] Those which had been authorized by Paul III and Clement VII were then compiled into a volume called *'Speculum Perfectionis'*.[3]

[1] Bull, *Ad uberes fructus,* March 10, 1526 (Wadding, *Annales Minorum,* XVI, 593-602; *Orbis Seraphicus,* II, 903-911).

[2] Bull, *Ad uberes fructus,* July 3, 1547 (Wadding, *o. c.,* XVIII, 435-460).

[3] Innocent XI, Bull, *Ecclesiae Catholicae,* June 28, 1686 (*Bull. Rom.,* XIX, 697).

The General Chapter of the First Order held at Rome under the title '*Pro Tertiariis et Chordigeris*', approved of these statutes and inculcated their use for all Tertiaries.[4] They were then published as accessory to, and as an explanation of, the Rule of Nicholas IV; because of their approval by Innocent XI they are commonly known as the '*Statuta Innocentiana*', of the *Statutes of Innocent XI*.

Consequently when Benedict XIII placed the Franciscan Secular Tertiaries under the jurisdiction of the Friars Minor, he simultaneously confirmed the approbation of his predecessors regarding these statutes, when he himself enjoined their use as a means of guidance for the Tertiaries.[5]

But these 'Statuta Innocentiana' seem to have fallen into disuse for the reason that, being accessory to the Rule of Nicholas IV, they were supplanted by that of Leo XIII, May 30, 1883. However since the *Ceremonial of the Third Order* approved through the S. C. of Rites June 18, 1883, demands that Tertiaries in their profession promise to observe the Rules of the Order according to the Rules of Leo XIII and Nicholas IV (*Ceremonial*, Art. IV); there is no reason why these statutes cannot be called into force in points of legislation which are not fully covered by the Rule of Leo XIII. Beyond this they have not the force of

[4] Antonius de Cipressa, *Regula sive Modus vivendi Fratrum de Poenitentia S. Francisci*, p. 41.

[5] "Injungimus * * * ministro generali * * * ut * * * Tertii Ordinis Congregationes saeculares * * * juxta constitutiones seu statuta a felicis recordationis Paulo III antecessore nostro approbata, vel secundum alia in speculo seraphico contenta atque directorium trium Ordinum inserta, necnon per recolendae memoriae Innocentios Papas XI [*Ecclesiae Catholicae*, June 28, 1686—*Bull. Rom.*, XIX, 690-699], XII [*Debitum pastoralis officii*, May 19, 1694—*o. c.*, XX, 631-648] et XIII [*Ordines et congregationes*, Jan. 13, 1724—*Chronologia hist-leg. Seraphici Ordinis*, III, part. II, 24 f] confirmata, quae etiam praesentium tenore renovamus et approbamus, confovere et moderari curet studeatque." (*Paterna Sedis Apostolicae*, Dec. 10, 1725, § 8—*Bull. Rom.*, XXII, 289).

law for nowhere in recent times are they authoritatively quoted as such. Besides Benedict XIII after enjoining the use of these statutes as quoted above, leaves it to the judgment of the Minister-General and his Chapter as to whether these shall be used or not: he grants them full authority to change anything which is not against the Rule and the sacred canons.[6] Moreover the General Constitutions of the Friars Minor (Leonine) omit any mention of these statutes and decree that the Tertiary congregations shall be governed according to the norms determined by the *'Definitorium Provinciale'*.[7] Although these Constitutions are approved only for the Friars Minor Leonine, on the other hand due to the fact that the three First Orders and the Third Order Regular, as already stated, and as affirmed by Pius X,[8] have equal power over the Tertiaries, their respective Provincial chapters also possess this authority. Neither can it be objected that Benedict XIII only granted this authority to the General Chapter, for a decree of the S. C. of Bishops and Regulars in 1761 expressly declared that this does not exclude other Superiors of the Order from legislative power in regard to the Third Order Secular.[9]

[6] "* * * nisi tamen eidem generali ministro et capituli generalis patribus aliud in Domino videbitur expedire: quibus propterea plenum jus ac libere auctoritatem ea innovandi, immutandi, augendi aut imminuendi, ac alia de caetero statuendi quae bonum dicti gregis regimen concernere possunt, dummodo tamen regulae praefatae sacrisque canonibus non adversentur, perpetuis temporibus facimus atque largimur." (§ 8.)

[7] *Regulae et Constitutiones Generales O. F. M.*, n. 686.

[8] "Ministri Generales triplicis familiae pari sunt potestate in Ordinem Tertium." (Cf. above, p. 96 f).

[9] "Breve Benedictinum non obstare quominus etiam Superiores Provinciales edere valeant particulares Ordinationes pro sui Tertii Ordinis meliori regimine, dummodo Regulae et Apostolicis Constitutionibus non adversentur."—Jan. 17, 1761 (Stein, *Tertius Ordo Franciscalis*, p. 63

Since then the Provincial Chapter has the authority of enacting particular statutes which are not against the Rule and papal decrees, it is consequent that Tertiaries and Directors are not free to decide whether they shall be observed or not, but rather that they have the force of law.

ARTICLE II

Erection of Franciscan Tertiary Sodalities

§ 1. Definition

Fraternal charity and mutual help toward one another as embodied in the Rule of Leo XIII presupposes a close union and close cooperation of Tertiaries, which is best brought about by grouping the Tertiaries into local associations or corporations. These local organizations, according to canon 702 §2 are called Sodalities: Si tertius saecularis Ordo in plures associationes dividatur, harum quaelibet legitime constituta dicitur sodalitas tertiariorum. A Sodality may thus be defined: An association of Tertiaries, legitimately erected according to the Rule, into a moral person organically constituted. It is called an association, for this is the specific term used by the Code to denote a juridically organized group of laity.

A Sodality of the Third Order Secular of St. Francis is

f); Antonius de Cipressa, p 43, in quoting this decree has the words 'Superiores *Discalceati*' instead of 'Superiores *Provinciales*' as in Stein; however granting the correctness of the decree of Antonius de Cipressa, *o. c.*, this would include the Provincials to say the least, for both authors agree on the word '*Superiores*' which is in the plural and therefore comprehends Superiors othen than the Ministers-General, namely the Provincials.

a moral person,[1] for it has the essentials of such a juridical quality: No association is recognized in the Church unless it has been erected or approved by legitimate authority.[2] Nor does an association become a moral person unless a legitimate ecclesiastical Superior has given it a formal decree of erection.[3] But since Religious Superiors cannot validly erect a Sodality of Tertiaries without the consent of the Ordinary of the place,[4] and this consent, according to can. 686 §3, must be in writing,[5] it follows that according to can. 100, a Sodality of the Third Order Secular is a moral person.

Besides a Tertiary Sodality possesses the other requisites of a moral collegiate person:[6] by its very nature it is perpetual,[7] and it is organically constituted with its director, officials and administrators.[7*]

§ 2. Requisite Permission for the Erection of Sodalities

For the valid erection of any association, the permission of the ordinary of the place is required, even though an apostolic privilege to the contrary has been proven; this permission must be in writing under pain of invalidity, unless the

[1] "In Ecclesia, praeter personas physicas, sunt etiam personae morales, publica auctoritate constitutae, quae distinguuntur in personas collegiales et non collegiales." (can. 99) "Catholica Ecclesia et Apostolica Sedes moralis personae rationem habent ex ipsa ordinatione divina; caeterae inferiores personae morales in Ecclesia eam sortiuntur ex speciali compententis Superioris ecclesiastici concessione data per formale decretum ad finem religiosum vel caritativum." (can. 100, § 1).

[2] Can. 686, § 1.

[3] Can. 687; 100, § 1.

[4] " . . . Superiores religiosi . . . nequeunt sodalitatem tertiariorum valide erigere sine consensu Ordinarii loci, ad normam can. 686, § 3." (can. 703, § 2.)

[5] "Licet privilegium cincessum probetur, semper tamen, nisi aliud in ipso privilegio cautum sit, requiritur ad validitatem erectionis consensus Ordinarii loci scripto datus; . . . " (can. 686, § 3).

[6] Cf. Chelodi, *Jus de Personis,* nn. 97-100.

[7] Cf. *A. S. S.,* XXVI, 485-498.

[7*] Cf. Ceremonial of the Third Order. These various offices are treated throughout this dissertation.

apostolic privilege provides otherwise.[8] Canon 703 §2 places Sodalities of the Third Order Secular under this law by demanding that they cannot validly be erected without the permission of the ordinary of the place which must be observed according to can. 686 §3; since the Friars Minor have no privilege stating expressly that the permission of the ordinary of the place need not be in writing, their Sodalities are bound by this law. Therefore in order validly to erect a Sodality of the Franciscan Third Order Secular, the permission of the ordinary of the place must be obtained in writing; this written consent is known as a *formal decree of erection.*[9]

Up to Jan. 31, 1893, this consent was required neither for validity or liceity;[10] on this date the S. C. of Indulgences decreed that the permission of the ordinary of the place was necessarily (necessario) required.[11] Some authors are of the opinion that this decree rendered the consent of the ordinary of the place only necessary for liceity,[12] while the more prominent canonists who treat this question, consider the decree

[8] Can. 686, § 3.

[9] Can. 100, § 1.

[10] In a decision of the S. C. of Bishops and Regulars March 13, 1744, it was stated that in a particular Church the Friars Minor were not (*negative*) allowed to erect Tertiary Congregations without the consent of the ordinary of the place. (*Fontes*, n. 1860 ad VI); but this decision was for a particular place and was withdrawn the following year: "Praevio recessu a decisis, *affirmative*."—*S. C. of Bishops and Regulars*, May 2, 1745 (*Analecta Juris Pontificii*, Sèrie 14 (1875), 844).

[11] "Utrum ad erigendam novam Congregationem Tertii Ordinis sive in Ecclesiis Regularium sive non Regularium necessario requiritur consensus Ordinarii loci"? Response: "Affirmative." (*A. S. S.*, XXV, 506-509, ad II.)

[12] Genarri, *Quistioni Canoniche*, n. 33; Beringer, *die Ablässe*, II, nn. 360 f; Stein, *Tertius Ordo Franciscalis*, p. 39 f; Mocchegiani, *Collectio Indulgentiarum*, nn. 1592 f; Mileta, *Trattato Giuridico sul Terz' Ordine Secolare*, p. 46; Tachy, *Les Tiers Ordres*, n. 37, makes no comment on this decree.

as containing an invalidating clause.[13] Arguing from the word *'necessario'* and the weight of authors, the writer is of the opinion that this consent was required for validity; certainly the consent did not need to be in writing for the decree mentions nothing of this.

The necessity of obtaining the consent of the ordinary of the place for the erection of a Third Order Sodality is entirely in keeping with the present canon law which states that when permission to erect a religious house is granted by the ordinary of the place, an association which is proper to that religion may also be erected in that place without further permission of the local ordinary, provided that this association be not an organically constituted body;[14] but a Sodality of the Third Order Secular is an organically constituted body with its director and Tertiary officials: therefore the reason for the distinction in regard to the necessity of obtaining the consent of the ordinary of the place for its erection.

The Vicar General without a special delegation, or the Vicar Capitular cannot give permission to erect Third Order Sodalities.[15]

§ 3. Persons with Jurisdiction to erect and direct Third Order Sodalities

In a previous article it was outlined that the Friars Minor, through the concession of many pontiffs, possess ordinary spiritual jurisdiction over the Franciscan Third Order Secular. The question may be asked: What members of the

[13] Piat, *Praelectiones Juris Regularis,* II, Q. 71; Vermeersch, *De Religiosis Institutis et Personis,* I, n. 537; Bondini, *De Privilegio Exemptionis,* p. 73; Prümmer, *Manuale Juris Ecclesiastici,* II, p. 314; Wernz, *Jus Decretalium,* III, 2, n. 718.

[14] Can. 686, § 3.

[15] Can. 686, § 4.

Order of Friars Minor, or rather, what office must one necessarily possess in that Order, that one automatically enjoys authority to erect and govern Sodalities of the Third Order? The answer, from various papal pronouncements and decrees is that this authority is enjoyed by the Ministers-general anywhere in the world, by the Provincials in their provinces, and by the local Superiors in their territory or district.

Benedict XIII, in completely subjecting the Tertiaries to the authority of the Friars Minor, enjoins the Minister-General to erect congregations everywhere, either through himself or through his commissaries; they have authority of investing with the habit, instructing in the Rule, punishing transgressions, presiding at all meetings, and performing the office of visitation.[16]

Descending to particulars he demands that the Tertiaries, under pain of expulsion from the Order, shall obey the Minister-General, Provincials and Guardians in all things; the Tertiaries shall consider them as their superiors in the same manner as Francis is venerated as the head and founder of the whole Order; if they fail to do this these same Superiors may deprive them of the habit and thus they loose all right to the privileges of the Order. Although in this Bull the pontiff does not expressly concede to the Provincials and the Guardians the authority of erecting Tertiary Sodalities, its implicit concession could not be more clear, for in order that these same Tertiaries be obedient to them, it is necessary that the Sodality be erected, and that they are professed therein as Tertiaries.[17]

This jurisdiction existed in these superiors even before

[16] Bull, *Paterna Sedis Apostolicae,* Dec. 10, 1725, §§ 7-8 (*Bull. Rom.,* XXIII, 285-294).

[17] "Tertiarii saeculares primarium generalem honorent, ejusque secundarios delegatos, sive provinciales, sive guardianos, aut etiam commissarios visitatores, tamquam suos legitimos et veros superiores vene-

the time of Benedict XIII, for the *Statutes of Innocent XI* (which enjoyed papal approbation),[18] gave the Guardian authority over Tertiary Sodalities in his territory. In particular, the Statutes mention that this authority rests with the provincial in his Province and the Guardian throughout his district; the Tertiaries in isolated places (where there are no Franciscan Convents) should be provided for by a *delegated* secular priest, always saving the right of the Guardian;[19] the Guardian is called the *ordinary* throughout his district.[20]

Benedict XIII in the Bull, *Ratio Apostolici Ministerii,* June 23, 1726, grants the Minister-General of the Friars Minor Capuchin and his secondary Superiors (that is, the Provincials and at least Guardians), complete authority to erect the Third Order Secular of St. Francis, receive profession, instruct in the Rule, in one word to subject the Tertiaries completely to their authority.[21]

rentur ita ut ipsorum judicio in dubiis et controversiis circa regulam et statuta se conforment, atque in iis omnibus, quae concernunt Ordinem ipsum, nec regulac sunt contraria, illis pareant et obediant: quod si secus fecerint, ab eisdem cassari atque habitu spoliari possint, immo nullis proinde gratiis et privilegiis gaudere decernimus et jubemus." (§ 7.) It cannot be objected that the provincials and guardians enjoy only delegated authority, for the word '*delegatos*', as is apparent from the context, is used in the sense that the Superiors are *representatives* of the Minister-General in their office. Besides, the word '*delegatos*' is used in apposition to the word '*commissarios*', the latter of which indeed seems to indicate a commission or a delegation.

[18] Cf. above chap. VIII, Art. I.

[19] Ad Cap. XVI.

[20] Ad Cap. XVIII.

[21] "* * * Tertiarii * * * ministro generali Ordinis fratrum Minorum beati Francisci qui Capuccini appelantur, * * * et ab ejus secundariis ministris * * * in rebus spiritualibus * * * omnino dependent * * *" (§ 1) "Statuimus * * * ministro generali Ordinis fratrum Minorum * * * qui Capuccini appelantur, et secundariis superioribus ab eodem ministri dependentibus, * * * convenire et competere * * * erigere, instituere et fundare Tertium Ordinem beati Francisci * * * pro per-

The pontiff uses the same words in effect when he gives this jurisdiction to the 'Minister-General of the Friars Minor Conventual and his secondary Superiors',[22] and to the same Superiors of the Third Order Regular.[23] The words 'Secondary Superiors' must of necessity have reference to the Provincials and Guardians to say the least: the context itself indicates this.[24]

Benedict XIV defending the rights and privileges of the *'Fratres Minores Discalceati et Recollecti'* concerning their jurisdiction over the Tertiaries, declares that all who are legitimate sons of St. Francis have equal authority over them; their Superiors and Guardians may erect the Third Order wherever they have founded a convent.[25]

In his *Rule for the Third Order,* Leo XIII empowers the Guardian to delegate a priest for the canonical visitation, which is the same as saying that he has ordinary jurisdiction.[26] In the *Ceremonial of the Third Order,* the Guardian

sonis saecularibus utriusque sexus, atque hujusmodi Tertii Ordinis professoribus beati Francisci scapulare sive habitum cum cingulo conferre, in rebus spiritualibus dirigere, in tertia regula beati Francisci observanda privatim et publice docere et instruere, * * *" (§ 3) (*Bull. Rom.*, XXII, 367-370).

[22] Bull, *Singularis Devotio,* July 3, 1726 (*o. c.,* 370-373).

[23] Bull, *Exponi nobis,* Sept. 30, 1729 (*o. c.,* 856-858).

[24] "Jamvero Superiores *secundarii* in Ordine fratrum Minorum Capucin., uti et Observantium et Conventualium, post Ministrum Generalem, sunt *Provinciales* et *Guardiani:* igitur ad hos respective pertinet recipere ad habitum et professionem Tertii Ordinis, videlicet ad Ministrum Generalem in toto Ordine, ad Provincialem in propria Provincia, ad Guardianum in propria *Guardiniana,* seu districtu, nec non ad eos, quibus id commissum constiterit; sed illis ex dispositione *juris,* istis ex commissione *hominis,* seu delegatione Generalium, Provincialium, et Guardiniaorum, pro tempore."—Antonius de Cipressa, *o. c.,* p. 38 (the italics in this quotation belong to the original author); cf. Hilarius Parisiensis, Liber Tertii Ordinis, p. 228-235.

[25] Bull, *Laudabile,* Aug. 2, 1745 (*Bull. Rom. Continuatio,* I, 547-550).

[26] *Rule* III, § 3.

is specifically mentioned as not only having authority to erect Sodalities (Art. VII), but also as presiding at all official functions of the Sodality.

Pius X, inculcating a more diffusive spread of the Third Order, recommends that Tertiary Sodalities be erected, not only where Franciscan Religious are established, but also in the parishes under the care of the secular clergy, with the necessary delegation of the Franciscan Superiors, but *'salvo semper jure et officio Praelatorum Ordinis Primi',*[37] namely, the Ministers-General, the Provincials, the Guardians and other local Superiors.[38] Neither can it be said that Pius X excludes the Third Order Regular from this jurisdiction, for: a) the omission of any mention of the Third Order Regular is easily explained by the fact that this Brief is addressed to members of the First Order; b) a privilege such as the Third Order Regular enjoys over the Secular Tertiaries is considered to be perpetual unless the opposite is

[37] Brief, *Tertium Franciscalium Ordinem,* Sept. 8, 1912 (*A. A. S.*, IV [1912], 484 f).

[38] "Praelati inter regulares, supremi sunt generales, medii sunt provinciales, et infimi sunt Superiores locales, videlicet priores, rectores, guardiani, et hujusmodi, et vicarii in capite, scilicet non habentes in suis conventibus superiores; isti enim omnes sunt vere praelati cum habeant in suos subditos jurisdictionem quasi-episcopalem." Ferraris, s. v. *Regularis Praelatus,* n. 3; cf. can. 110; 198, § 1; *CpR.*, II [1921], pp. 114 f; Vermeersch, *De Religiosis Institutis et Personis,* I, n. 412; Maroto, *Institutiones Juris Canonici,* I, n. 485; Vermeersch-Creusen, *Epitome,* I, n. 201; Ferreres, *Institutiones Canonicae,* I, n. 245; Ojetti, *Synopsis Rerum Moralium et Juris Pontificii,* s. v. *Praelatus Regularis;* the Minister-General, provincials and guardians are known as prelates in the Order of Friars Minor—cf. passim Grecchio, *Manuale Praelati Franciscani; Constitutiones O. M. Conv.; Regula et Constitutiones Generales O. F. M.; Regula et Constitutiones Fratrum Minorum Capuccinorum; Regula del Terz' Ordine Claustrale di S. Francesco D'Assisi;* Lyszcarczyk, *Compendium Privilegiorum Regularium,* p. 73 f, note 1; in particular the *Regula et Constitutiones Generales O. F. M.*, n. 572 expressly denote the Guardian as a prelate.

evident:[29] there is nothing in this Brief to prove that it was revoked; c) when the pontiff in this same Brief wishes to exclude the Third Order Regular he makes special mention of it: thus a short space after the above quotation, when speaking of conventions of the Third Order Secular he states 'religious *only* (dumtaxat) of the First Order can call conventions and preside at them'; hence the former words giving jurisdiction to erect and direct Sodalities are given in a *demonstrative* manner—the latter in giving jurisdiction to convoke conventions are given in a *taxative* manner; therefore the Third Order Regular retains its jurisdiction of erecting and directing Sodalities. Far from divesting the Third Order Regular of this jurisdiction, more recent pontiffs have encouraged it: thus Benedict XV praises their efforts toward the Third Order Secular in the past, insists that it is their office to be at the head of (duces) the Secular Tertiaries, and sanctions this by giving indulgences for a specified time to these same Franciscan Seculars under their care.[30]

In the above-quoted Brief of Pius X, he indicates that the Prelates to which he refers are the Ministers-General, the Provincials, Guardians and the local Superiors, and at the same time indicates that their jurisdiction is territorially circumscribed, when he speaks of conventions of the Third Order Secular: "if the Tertiaries gather from a district, the custos or Guardian of the convent shall convoke them and preside at the convention; if from a province, the minister

[29] Cf. can. 4 and 70.

[30] Benedict XV, *Tertii Ordinis a Poenitentia*, Feb. 20, 1921 (*A. A. S.*, XIII [1921], 130 f).

provincial; if from many provinces; the Minister General of the Order; * * *"[51]

From the numerous decrees cited it is clear that the Friars Minor have authority to erect Tertiary Sodalities, receive into the Third Order and exercise complete spiritual care over them in so far as they are Tertiaries. This jurisdiction applies to the Ministers-General anywhere in the Order, the Provincials in their Provinces, and the Guardians in their districts—the latter are those who are canonically elected Superiors of a 'domus formata'.[52]

Due to the fact that the majority of the pontifical decrees give this authority to the Minister-General 'and his secondary Superiors', without specifying the exact nature of their office or the manner of their being placed in office, this authority resides equally in those who are Superiors of convents and residences which are not canonically called *'domus formatae'*; as also in those who legitimately succeed in office, due to the death or absence of the Guardian, according to the Constitutions of the respective Order.[53] This interpretation is also favored by Leo XIII, when in audience granted to the four Ministers-General of the First Order and the Third Order Regular, he expressly states that 'where

[51] "Religiosi dumtaxat ex Ordine Primo coetus seu conventus sodalium Ordinis Tertii cogant iisdemque praesideant; si sodales a districtu coeant, coenobii custos seu Guardianus; si e provincia, provincialis Minister; si e pluribus provinciis, Ordinis Minister generalis." (Brief, *Tertium Franciscalium Ordinem*, Sept. 8, 1912 (*A. A. S.*, I [1912], 584, n. I).

[52] Can. 488, 5°; *Regula et Constitutiones Generales O. F. M.*, nn. 315 f.

[53] Cf. *Regula et Constitutiones Generales O. F. M.*, nn. 579, 581; *Constitutiones O. F. M. Conv.*, Cap. VIII, Tit. XLIV; *Regula et Constitutiones O. F. M. Cap.*, nn. 156-159; *Regula del Terz' Ordine Claustrale di S. Francesco D'assisi*, p. 158, VI, wherein these temporary local Superiors are given the same local authority as the Guardians whom they supply.

there are no Franciscan Fathers, the Third Order should be promoted through *delegated* Directors';[34] in other words, *wherever* there is a Franciscan foundation, no matter of what nature it may be, *there* is authority to erect and direct Sodalities of the Third Order *without any delegation*—which erection and direction, from papal documents, belongs to the Superior of that community.

This jurisdiction, although ordinary, is not to be taken in the sense of canon 198, but rather in the general sense of canon 197 §1, i. e., that the Franciscan Superiors enjoy ordinary jurisdiction over the Tertiary Sodalities and their members only in their relation to the Third Order, i. e., in so far as they are Tertiaries. And since this jurisdiction is ordinary, it can be delegated to others of the Order of Friars Minor, or to both regular and secular clergy who do not belong to the Order; this delegation may be either in whole or in part.[35] Since this delegation to erect Sodalities in most instances is given for a particular place and is therefore not universal (ad universitatem negotiorum) it cannot be subdelegated unless such a subdelegation was expressly mentioned in the delegation; however if a universal delegation were given (e. g. to a bishop of a diocese), this delegation could be subdelegated.[36] A universal or a particular delegation would not cease *resoluto jure delegantis et re integra,* unless such a stipulation were made in the delegation.[37]

If a delegation were given to a pastor to erect and direct a Sodality, the latter part of the delegation should ordinarily be understood in the light of canon 58 so that it would be

[34] July 7, 1883 (*A. M.* II, 111; Fleming, *Leonis XIII Acta ad III Ordinem Spectantia*, p. 36); cf. also the Letter of the Secretary of State of Leo XIII to the Italian bishops, Sept. 30, 1882, which has the same tenor (Fleming, *o. c.*, p. 30).

[35] Can. 199, § 1.

[36] Can. 199, §§ 3-4.

[37] Cf. can. 207, § 2.

given *ratione officii,* and therefore the successor in office would be able to continue receiving members and performing the office of Director or Moderator without the necessity of recurring to the Franciscan Superiors for faculties. The very nature of a Third Order Sodality as a moral person erected perpetually (*persona moralis, natura sua, perpetua est*)[38] postulates this interpretation of the delegation.

From the papal documents cited it is certain that the jurisdiction of the Friars Minor is territorial in regard to the erection of a Sodality and the reception of members into the same, although Gennari believes that the Franciscan Superiors can validly receive outside the limits of this territory provided they do not ascribe them to a Sodality;[39] such Tertiaries who do not belong to a Sodality are known as solitaries (*Solitarii*). In the opinion of the writer, this view is tenable for: a) the various papal pronouncements in speaking of the jurisdiction of the Franciscan Superiors as being territorial always have reference to their authority in regard to Sodalities, i. e., their erection and the reception of Tertiaries into these Sodalities; b) canon 703 §2 allows the Religious Superiors to receive Tertiaries such as Gennari describes into the Third Order and at the same time does not limit their jurisdiction territorially in this regard; the same may be said of a decision of the S. C. of Indulgences July 14, 1891, which allows those who have faculties to receive into the Third Order without ascribing these same Tertiaries to a Sodality: this decision does not speak of any territorial limitation.[40]

[38] Can. 102, § 1.

[39] Gennari, Quistioni Theologico-Morali, n. 336.

[40] *A. S. S.*, XXIV, 448; cf. can. 68 and 50—this interpretation does not come under any of the restrictions of these canons: therefore a wide interpretation may be used. Stein, *Tertius Ordo Franciscalis*, p. 59 f, favors the opposite view.

The opinion that a Tertiary Sodality can be erected which is comprised entirely of novices[41] seems to be without sufficient foundation. Obviously a Third Order Sodality, as the name implies, must be comprised of at least three professed Tertiaries (for they do not become Tertiaries until they are professed), and it is doubtful if the law could be drawn to such a point where novices could be called Tertiaries. Granted that the ordinary of the place would give his written consent for such an erection, no such jurisdiction has been given to the Friars Minor to erect such a moral person and to receive members into it. Therefore it could not be called a Third Order Sodality, and if it is not, then it is beside the question in view. The argument that religious novices are subject to the Superiors of the religious institute in which they are to become professed,[42] confirms, rather than weakens, this view for, a) Franciscan Tertiary novices *are* subject to the Franciscan Superiors (or their delegate) *in ordine ad futuram professionem,* without the necessity of forming a Sodality; b) religious novices cannot form a domus formata,[43] and *a pari,* Tertiary novices cannot be formed into a moral person known as a *Third Order* Sodality.

Neither can it be said that such novices are deprived of the insight into the purpose and activities of the Third Order which is necessary for their ultimate acceptance of the Rule in profession: without being formed into a Sodality they must of necessity be instructed in the Rule, and can observe all the regulations of the Third Order with the exception of the election of the officers of the Sodality, and the consequent administration of the funds of a Sodality as a moral person —two considerations which will have little bearing on their

[41] Stein, *Tertius Ordo Franciscalis,* p. 26.

[42] Can. 561 § 2.

[43] Can. 488, 5°.

final selection of the Third Order as a means of acquiring Christian perfection.

§ 4. Method of Erection—Translation—Extinction.

The method of erecting a Third Order Sodality is given in the Ceremonial of the Third Order, Article VII. There is nothing mentioned however, as to the necessity of this form being observed under pain of nullity or liceity: therefore any act of competent authority with the intention of erecting a Sodality would suffice for validity.[44] But since a Sodality is erected into a moral person, this erection becomes an act of public authority, and it is therefore necessary that public proof be available.[45] Thus this proof of the existence of a Sodality can be either through a decree of erection—which method is advised by Benedict XIII[46]—or through an enactment of the one who has erected the Sodality, with the officials of the Sodality as witnesses: this method is given in the *Ceremonial of the Third Order,* Article VII.[47]

Tertiary Sodalities are not bound by the *lex loci,* which does not allow two associations in the same place. Clement XII gave this concession to the Friars Minor Capuchin when he stated that they could erect Tertiary Sodalities even

[44] Cf. Gennari, *Quistioni Theologico-Morali,* n. 336.

[45] Can. 99; cf. Chelodi, *Jus de Personis,* n. 98.

[46] Bull, *Paterna Sedis Apostolicae,* Dec. 10, 1725, § 8 (*Bull. Rom.,* XXII, 289)—"Injungimus * * * generali ministro * * * ut * * * Tertii Ordinis congregationes saeculares, * * * *per patentes litteras* * * * erigere * * * curet studeatque."

[47] After the erection, he who has erected the Sodality together with the officials shall deposit the testimony of the erection in the archieves, which may be drawn up in this manner: "Anno Domini * * *, die * * * infracscriptus ego N. Guardianus (vel Visitator, aut Director, aut Sacerdos facultatibus legitimis a N. receptis munitus) erexi Congregationem Tertii Ordinis sub invocatione et patrocinio S. N., in loco N., Testibus N. N. presentibus. In quorum fidem cum Testibus subscripsi."

where others already are founded;[48] this privilege was later acknowledged by the S. C. of Indulgences, Jan. 31, 1893, when it decided that Franciscan Third Order Sodalities are not bound by the *lex loci* as laid down by Clement VIII.[49]

On account of diversity of language, age, sex, etc., more than one Sodality of the Third Order may be erected in the same church or chapel; each may have its own proper Director and Officials, and enjoys all the indulgences and privileges, in the same manner as if there were but one Sodality in the place.[50] Since the Third Order is not bound by the law laid down for Confraternities that they must be erected in a church, a public or a semi-public oratory,[51] it follows that where there is lack of such a place, any permanent place may be used.

After the erection, the erector shall nominate, i. e., institute the officials of the Sodality,[52] although this is not necessary for the validity of the erection; this was decided by the S. C. of Indulgences, Nov. 14, 1842, in regard to Confra-

[48] "* * * Ministro generali Ordinis Capuccinorum et secundariis superioribus ab eo dependentibus, * * * conveniat et competat in quocumque loco, civitate, provincia et regno, *etiam ubi alii Tertiarii ejusdem Ordinis jam reperiuntur,* instituere et fundare praefatum Tertium Ordinem * * * " (Bull, *Apostolicae servitutis,* July 23, 1735, § 1—*Bull. Rom.,* XXIV, 61).

[49] "An Tertius Ordo Saecularis S. Francisci teneatur lege illa a Clemente Papa VIII in Constitutione "*Quaecumque*" d. d. 7 Decembris 1604 statuta, qua praecipitur unam tantum Confraternitatem et Congregationem ejusdem nominis et instituti erigi posse in singulis civitatibus et oppodis"? Response: "Negative." (*M. E.,* 8, Ser. I, vol. VIII, 33 f); the *A. S. S.,* XXV, 506 quotes the Constitution of Clement VIII as "*Quaeitur*"; this is evidently wrong—cf. this Const. in the *Fontes,* n. 192.

[50] *S. C. of Iudulgences,* March 8, 1905 (*M. E.,* 7, Ser. II, vol. XVII, 204).

[51] Can. 712, § 1.

[52] *Ceremonial of the Third Order,* Art. VII.

ternities,[63] and although the present question concerns a Sodality of the Third Order Secular, the parity between the two is apparent in reference to their juridical condition as a moral person, and their rights as well as privileges in reference to the election of officials and administrators.

All erections of Sodalities of the Franciscan Third Order which had been invalidly performed in good faith, were granted a sanation by a rescript of the S. C. of Religious, Jan. 8, 1924; the rescript was executed Jan. 19, 1924.[64]

Translation of a Sodality. The principles regarding the translation of Confraternities from one place to another in the diocese may also be applied here. Confraternities as moral persons certainly possess this right,[65] which may be used after the consent of the ordinary of the place has been obtained,[66] and in the case of confraternities which are aggregated to a certain religion (which is precisely the case with Franciscan Third Order Sodalities), the consent of the Religious Superior is required;[67] the consent of the majority of the members, given collegiately, is also required.[68] A Confraternity thus translated retains all its indulgences,[69] not however those which were granted solely in connection with

[63] "An necesse sit sub poena nullitatis ut administratores confraternitatis eligantur?" Response: "Negative, quia administratores electio erit tantum ad bonum Sodalitatum regimen, minime vero ad validitatem erectionis necessaria."—ad II (*Decreta Authentica S. C. Indulg.*, n. 312).

[64] *A. M.*, XLIII, 47.

[65] Wernz, *Jus Decretalium,* III. 2., n. 716; Cocchi, *Commentarium,* IV, n. 189, (e).

[66] Can. 719, § 1; *o. c.*

[67] Can. 719, § 2.

[68] Wernz, *l. c.;* Piat, *Praelectiones Juris Regularis,* II, Q. 79; Ferraris, s. v. *Confraternitas,* Art. I, n. 57; can. 101, § 1, 1°.

[69] *S. C. of Indulgences,* Feb. 16, 1739 (*Decreta Authentica S. C. Indulg.*, n. 126); March 15, 1852, ad II (*o. c,* n. 358); Wernz, *l. c.;* Piat, *l. c.*

the place from which the Confraternity was to be transferred (*ratione loci*);[60] the rights and obligations regarding the administration of the goods are also transferred, except regarding those goods which have been given by the donors, by reason of the place from which the Confraternity is transferred (ratione derelictae ecclesiae).[61]

Due to the fact that Third Order Sodalities agree perfectly as moral persons with this specific legislation regarding the translation of Confraternities, canon 20 may be aptly applied here so that this legislation has equal reference to Sodalities of the Third Order Secular.

Extinction of a Sodality. A Sodality of the Third Order Secular is by its very nature perpetual, and therefore does not cease to exist by the mere will of its members, for it is erected by *public* ecclesiastical authority, and hence cannot be dissolved by *private* authority.[62]

Canon law provides two methods of extinction—

a) *By legitimate ecclesiastical authority*: it is logical that the Church, which sanctions all ecclesiastical corporations, may also suppress them; for this reason the supreme pontiff, as head of all ecclesiastical bodies, may suppress it, as also the ordinary of the place for grave reasons, and saving recourse to the Holy See, i. e., the S. C. of Religious.[63] For the reason that a Tertiary Sodality is perpetually erected in the diocese for the good of souls, it does not seem that it can be suppressed by the Franciscan Superiors without the consent of the ordinary of the place; the very reason for its

[60] Wernz, *l. c.;* cf. Fanfani, *De Indulgentiis,* n. 3, p. 5.

[61] Wernz, *l. c.;* Piat, *l. c.;* Ferreres, *Institutiones Canonicae,* I, n. 990.

[62] Wernz, *o. c.,* n. 717; Ferreres, *La Confraternite,* n. 360, in reference to confraternities as moral persons, which is applicable to the present question through can. 20; Putzer, *Commentarium in Facultates Apostolicas,* p. 342, holds the opposite view, although giving no reasons for his opinion.

[63] Can. 102, § 1; 699, § 1; 251, § 1.

existence in the diocese is due to the consent of the ordinary of the place without which it cannot be erected.[64] Certainly it cannot be *arbitrarily* dissolved by the Franciscan Superiors.[65]

b) *Extinction of a Sodality also takes place when a Sodality has had no members for a space of one hundred years:*[66] due to negligence on the part of those in authority, it could happen that a Sodality with a large membership gradually dwindles down. In order to revive such a Sodality, what is to be done? If the membership in the Sodality has not been entirely vacant for a period of one hundred years, then anyone with legitimate faculties, either ordinary or delegated, can revive the Sodality by admitting Tertiaries to membership without a new erection (having of course made certain of the former legitimate erection). The reason for this is that if only one member of a moral person remains, the rights of the entire moral person remain in him,[67] and there-

[64] Can. 703, § 2; Maroto, *Institutiones*, I, n. 464, note (1).

[65] *S. C. of Bishops and Regulars*, Aug. 25, 1893 (*A. S. S.*, XXVI, 485-498); Wernz, *o. c.*, n. 718.

[66] Can. 102, § 1. This canon is entirely of precode origin—In 1667 a Confraternity of the Rosary was erected in the town of 'Casalbuono'. For over a space of one hundred years there were no members, but in 1882 it was revived by a new erection and the reception of new members. However, in 1826 another Congregation of the 'B. V. M. Perdolentis' had been legitimately erected in the same town. The question of precedence arose, which was decided by the Congregation of the Council, July 24, 1886, in favor of the latter society (*A. S. S.*, XIX, 319-326). Although the principle of law is '*qui prior est tempore, potior est jure*' (*Regula Juris 53 in VI°*), the Congregation nevertheless computed the existence of the former Society only from the year 1882, for it had lost all rights as a moral person due to the fact that it had had no members for over a space of one hundred years.

[67] Can. 102, § 2; thus it can be seen that although at least three physical persons are required to *erect or constitute* a moral collegiate person (can. 100, § 2), on the other hand, since once erected it is perpetual (can. 102, § 1), its *continuance* can be embodied in but one person.

fore to revive such a Sodality, only new membership is required, not a new erection. A practical case of a revival without a new erection, would be that of a Sodality in whose decree of erection the pastor of the church, *pro tempore existentiae paroeciae,* had been designated as Director. As long as the Sodality has not fallen into decay for a space of one hundred years, any pastor of this church can revive it by receiving new members, without the necessity of recurring to the Friars Minor for faculties of erection, or of receiving into the Third Order.[68]

A translation or an extinction is not had if the church in which the Sodality was erected is destroyed and erected within fifty years in the same place, and under the same or another title. The same can be said if the church where the Sodality is erected is transferred from the care of the regular clergy to the secular, or vice versa, or if the church has been profaned and again restored to use.[69]

Article III

The Government of Sodalities

§ 1. Membership in the Third Order

Having treated of the nature and purpose of the Third Order as well as the requisites for the erection of its Sodalities, the question concerning its members follows logically in order. Uniformity and order in any society always postulates norm and restriction regarding its members, which in the present case may be divided into two classes: the restrictions of Canon law, and the restrictions of the Rule of the Third Order.

a) *The restrictions of canon law:* Those who have taken

[68] Cf. can. 58.

[69] Wernz, *o. c.*, n. 717; can. 75 and 924, § 1.

vows in a religious institute cannot become Tertiaries,[1] although the words of this canon do not apply to those living in community life without vows.[2] This restriction regarding religious was made by the S. C. of Indulgences, July 16, 1887,[3] and the same Congregation, Jan. 31, 1893, declared that this former decree automatically cut off the membership of religious in the Third Order, even though they had been Secular Tertiaries at the time of its issuance;[4] if a religious is freed from his vows and returns to the world, his profession in the Third Order automatically revives.[5]

The decree of Jan. 31, 1893 (ad IX), confirmed by canon 705, does not allow Secular Tertiaries to belong to two Third Orders at the same time, nor to two Sodalities of the same Order; those who belonged to two Third Orders before this decree were allowed to choose the Order in which they wished to remain.[6]

For a just cause Tertiaries can transfer from one Third Order to another, or from one Sodality to another of the same Order.[7] The Third Order Secular of Dominic at Bologna has the Apostolic indult spoken of in canon 705, so that it can receive professed members of another Third Order, so that such Tertiaries belong to two Third Orders at the same time.[8]

[1] "Qui vota nuncupavit vel in perpetuum vel ad tempus in aliqua religione, nequit simul ad ullum tertium Ordinem pertinere, etsi eidem antea fuerit adscriptus." (can. 704, § 1).

[2] Vermeersch-Creusen, *Epitome*, I, n. 800; *S. C. of Indulgences*, July 16, 1887 (*A. S. S.*, XX, 111 f); Jan. 31, 1893, ad IV-VI (*o. c.*, XXV, 506-509).

[3] Cited in footnote 2.

[4] Cited in footnote 2.

[5] Can. 704, § 2.

[6] *S. C. of Indulgences*, June 21, 1893 (*A. S. S.*, XXV, 748).

[7] Can. 705.

[8] *S. C. of Indulgences*, Aug. 8, 1899 (*M. E.*, 1, Ser. II, vol. XI, 398).

Tertiaries who wish to take vows in a religious community may wear the habit of the Third Order until their religious profession, as well as take part in the indulgences and privileges of the Third Order.[10]

Public sinners, non-Catholics, those belonging to a condemned sect, as also those who are burdened with a censure of a notorious character, cannot validly be received into the Third Order.[11]

B) *The restrictions of the Rule*: Those who are under fourteen years of age cannot be admitted to profession; moreover candidates must be of good morals, peaceful,[12] faithful in the practice of the Catholic religion, and in their devotion to the Holy See.[13] Unless her confessor advises otherwise, a married woman cannot become a Tertiary without the consent of her husband.[14]

A novitiate of one year, which ordinarily begins with the reception of the habit (unless the director judges otherwise)[15] must be performed before one can validly be admitted to profession in the Third Order.[16] Since profession in the Third Order is a *new act*, the computation of the time of the novitiate must be made according to canon 34 §3, 3°

[10] *S. C. of Indulgences*, Jan. 31, 1893, ad V (*A. S. S.*, XXV, 506-509).

[11] Can. 693, § 1; Masonic societies are especially understood by 'condemned sects'—cf. *Fontes*, nn. 563 and 571; Quigley, *Condemned Societies*, pp. 89-93.

[12] The first Rule of the Third Order spoke of the obligation of restoring ill-gotten goods, and the necessity of being reconciled to one's enemies before being admitted to the Third Order. (X, 5-9.)

[13] *Rule of Leo XIII*, I, § 1; again the first Rule of the Order required that those suspected of heresy be cleared of this charge before the bishop: otherwise they could not enter the Order. (XI, 1.)

[14] *Rule of Leo XIII*, I, § 2.

[15] The form for imposing the habit is contained in the *Ceremonial of the Third Order*, Art. II.

[16] *Rule of Leo XIII*, I, § 4; *S. C. of Indulgences*, Jan. 30, 1896, ad V (*M. E.*, 9, Ser. I, vol. IX, 153).

and 5°,"[17] that is, if one begins the novitiate Jan. 26, 1929, he cannot validly emit profession until Jan. 27, 1930. In the event that a novice is placed in danger of death (in periculo mortis), any priest with faculties to hear confessions, provided one cannot be called who has the necessary faculties of reception, can validly receive the profession of the novice, even though the year of the novitiate be not completed; but his name is not to be written in the register of the Sodality until death, for if he recovers, he is to make profession anew, and then his name is written in the register of the Sodality.[18] This is the only reason allowed for valid dispensation from the full time of the novitiate.[19] If a novice either inadvertently or deliberately throws off the habit, i. e., the scapular and cord, his novitiate is not interrupted, provided the intention of becoming professed in the Third Order was not retracted.[20]

For good reasons one who has been admitted to the novitiate under the direction of one Franciscan obedience (e. g. Friars Minor Capuchin), may be professed in a Sodality under another obedience (e. g. Friars Minor Conventual).[21]

Before receiving to profession in the Third Order, the Director should decide on the worthiness of the novice with the advice of the Discretorium or officials of the Sodality,[22] although this advice is not necessary for the validity of the profession, since no Rule of the Third Order ever demanded this under pain of invalidity.

[17] Cf. Bakalarczyk, *De Novitiatu*, p. 113.

[18] *Ceremonial of the Third Order*, Art. III.

[19] *S. C. of Indulgences*, Jan. 30, 1896, ad V (*M. E.*, 9, Ser. I, vol. IX, 153).

[20] *S. C. of Indulgences*, March 4, 1903 (*A. S. S.*, XXXV, 637).

[21] *S. C. of Indulgences*, March 4, 1903, ad I (*A. S. S.*, XXXV, 637-639).

[22] *Statuta Innocentiana*, ad Cap. XIII; cf. below chap. VIII, Art. III, § 4.

In order to become a member of the Third Order, it is not necessary that one be ascribed to a Sodality,[23] although it is more commendable, and the purpose and end of the Third Order is certainly better attained by a closer union of the Tertiaries. The Tertiaries being united in local groups, there will be more room and occasion for correction on the part of the Franciscan Superiors; the care of the poor and the sick will be more properly attended to.[24]

In order to become a member of a Sodality, a professed Tertiary must have his name written in the register of the Sodality; this writing is necessary for validity.[25] If the inscription of the name of a professed Tertiary is omitted from the register of the Sodality, whether intentionally or accidentally, he nevertheless remains a member of the Third Order, but is known as a Solitarius, i. e., a Tertiary who has no membership in a local Sodality.

May a Solitarius take part in the indulgences and privileges of the Third Order? Canon 694 §2 stipulates that a Tertiary cannot become a member of a Sodality unless his name is written in the register; it is silent however as to whether local ascription is necessary in order to gain the indulgences of the Order. From this it is to be judged that local ascription has nothing to do with gaining the indulgences of the Order *as a whole*, for a) in the various indulgences which were granted to the Third Order by the Holy

[23] Can. 703, § 2; *S. C. of Indulgences*, July 14, 1891 (*A. S. S.*, XXIV, 448).

[24] Pius X, Brief, *Delectavit Nos*, Dec. 17, 1909 (*A. A. S.*, II [1910], 12).

[25] Can. 694, § 2; those who are absent cannot licitly be inscribed, although for good reasons, it seems that this can be dispensed with; one must freely and knowingly have his name inscribed in the Register of the Sodality: otherwise the inscription is invalid.—can. 693, § 2; cf. Chelodi, *Jus de Personis*, n. 300; Vermeersch-Creusen, *Epitome*, I, n. 791.

See, inscription in a Sodality was never mentioned as a requisite; the following or similar words were used: "Indulgences granted to Tertiaries";[26] b) from the words of canon 692 wherein the only necessary condition for gaining the indulgences and privileges of an association is that one must be a valid member of the same: an isolated Tertiary (Solitarius) is truly a valid member of the Third Order, and he therefore takes part in its indulgences and privileges.

On the other hand where membership in a Sodality is made a condition of gaining certain indulgences, or where particular indulgences are granted to a particular Sodality, it is evident that a Solitarius cannot take part in these; e. g., in the list of indulgences attached to the Rule, Leo XIII speaks of an indulgence granted to those who attend the monthly meeting of their Sodality.[27]

Stein[28] does not make such a distinction between gaining the indulgences and privileges pertaining to the Third Order as a whole, and those pertaining to Sodalities of the Order. He makes the general statement that inscription in the register of the Sodality has nothing to do with the gaining of indulgences, and to substantiate this he quotes a decree of the S. C. of the Holy Office, April 23, 1914.[29] But this decree has been abrogated in regard to Third Order Sodalities by subsequent canon law: a Sodality of the Third Order Secular is an association, and more specifically, a moral person;[30] in order validly to become a member of an association which is a moral person, inscription in its register is absolutely

[26] Thus Leo XIII in his list of indulgences attached to the Rule simply uses these words: "Tertiariis indulgentiam plenariam just sit * * *."

[27] I, 3.

[28] *Tertius Ordo Franciscalis,* p. 32.

[29] *A. A. S.,* VI [1914], 307 f.

[30] Cf. above Chap. VIII, Art. II, § 1; Fanfani, *De Jure Religiosorum,* n. 428.

necessary;[31] and further, that one may gain the indulgences and privileges which accrue to an association (which in the present case is a moral person), 'necesse est et sufficit, ut quis in eam valide receptus sit * * *';[32] this certainly contains an invalidating clause,[33] therefore since a Tertiary who has not had his name written in the register of the Sodality, is not a valid member thereof, neither can he partake in its indulgences and privileges.

Consequently, in order to partake of the indulgences and privileges pertaining to Sodalities of the Third Order Secular of St. Francis, one must have his name written in the register of the Sodality; hence a distinction must be made between these benefits granted to the Third Order *as a whole,* and those granted to *Sodalities* of the Third Order. For these reasons, if a Tertiary wished to become a member of a Sodality of the Third Order, and his name was not written in the register, even though it were through neglect or inadvertence, he cannot partake in the indulgences, rights and privileges of a Sodality.[34]

All admissions to the reception of the habit and to profession in the Third Order which had been invalid through essential defects committed in good faith, were granted a sanation by a rescript of the S. C. of Religious, Jan 8, 1924; the rescript was executed Jan. 19, 1924.[35]

Dismissal from the Third Order. Although profession in

[31] Can. 694, § 2.

[32] Can. 692.

[33] "Legitime receptus et non expulsus, hoc solo titulo fruitur associationis juribus, privilegiis, indulgentiis aliisque gratiis spiritualibus." (Vermeersch-Creusen, *Epitome,* I, n. 793; Cocchi, *Commentarium,* IV, n. 178, states that it is absolutely essential (omnino ac essentialiter) that one be validly received into an association in order to partake of its indulgences and privileges.

[34] Cf. Piat, *Praelections Juris Regularis,* II, Q. 71.

[35] *A. M.,* XLIII, 47.

the Third Order is made for the term of one's life,[36] on the other hand it would be illogical, and the very purpose of the Third Order would be frustrated if a recalcitrant member could not be dismissed, who by his life not only refused to observe the Rule for himself, but was also an occasion of scandal and laxity to other Tertiaries. Therefore the first Rule of the Order, while insisting on the perpetuity of the promises made in profession, at the same time gave the fraternity the right of expelling incorrigible members.[37]

A Tertiary may be dismissed for a just cause, according to the statutes of the Order;[38] the Rule of Leo XIII determines this cause to be just when a member of the Sodality remains disobedient after a third admonition.[39] For more serious defections, as in canon 696 § 2, members may be dismissed after one admonition, *'salvo jure recursus ad Ordinarium'*, that is the Franciscan major Superiors.[40]

Due to the fact that the Provincial with the Definitorium can enact particular statutes for Third Order Sodalities of his province,[41] in these same statutes provision may also be made for reasons of dismissal which are not contained in the

[36] The first Rule of the Order makes this provision: "De hac fraternitate et de iis quae hic continentur nemo exire valeat nisi religionem ingrediatur." (X, 2.) "Ordinamus statuentes ut nullus post ipsius fraternitatis ingressum de eadem egredi valeat ad saeculum reversurum." (*Rule of Nicholas IV*, II.)

[37] "Incorrigibiles fratres et sorores a fraternitate ejecti iterum in ea nullo modo recipiatur, nisi saniori parti fratrum placuerit." (XI, 3.)

[38] Can. 696, § 1.

[39] "Sodales nec obedientes et noxii iterum et tertium admoneantur oficii sui: ni pareant, excedere Ordine jubeantur." (III, § 4.)

[40] That the Franciscan major Superiors are comprehended is evident from the fact that the Provincial is Superior over all Tertiary Sodalities in his province, and the Minister-General over all in the Order. § 3 of the same canon indicates this by distinguishing the ordinary mentioned in that paragraph as 'Ordinarius *loci*'.

[41] Cf. above chap. VIII, Art. I.

Rule itself.[42] It is evident that those who govern the local Sodalities, whether by ordinary or delegated authority, have the right to dismiss the Tertiaries; this authority is also vested in the one who performs the canonical visitation.[43] Therefore the Director, or Moderator, have the right to dismiss even though the statutes mention nothing in this regard; this applies also to the ordinary of the place.[44]

Since nothing is mentioned in this canon concerning the reasons for dismissal, but simply gives this authority to the Superiors of Sodalities, it implicitly gives them the right of determining in particular cases, what reasons shall be considered as sufficiently grave to warrant dismissal. The Rule (III § 4) also implies this in these simple words: "Sodales nec obedientes . . . excedere Ordine jubeantur."—which disobedience must logically be determined by those in authority. Thus sufficient reason for dismissal would be repeated defection from those principles which Pius X declared should be followed by Tertiaries.[45]

Dismissal from the Sodality also implies dismissal from the Order,[46] although it would seem that for such offenses as failure to attend the meetings prescribed, or neglect of interest in the activities of the Sodality etc., would really not come under the heading of disobedience, and while giving warrant for dismissal from the Sodality, yet would hardly be sufficient reason for rejection from the Order, provided

[42] Cf. 696, § 1.

[43] Cf. *Rule of Leo XIII*, chap. III.

[44] Can. 696, § 3.

[45] "* * * Tertii Ordinis institutum in hoc consistere ut sodales evangelicae perfectionis praecepta in cotidianum usum ipsi deducant, et christianae vitae exemplar ceteris ad imitandum proponant."—Brief, Tertium Franciscalium Ordinem, Sept. 8, 1912 (*A. A. S.*, IV [1912], 585).

[46] "Sodales nec obedientes * * * excedere Ordine jubeantur." (*Rule of Leo XIII*, III, § 4.)

the general Rules of the Order had been observed.

Since profession in the order is for the term of one's life, a Tertiary cannot freely relinquish it without the acceptance of those in authority; but even if the resignation were not accepted, such a Tertiary would loose all right to the indulgences and privileges of the Order.[47] For reinstatement (if such a term may be used) of such a negligent Tertiary in the Order and in its indulgences and privileges, it is only necessary that the scapular and cord be reassumed—a second profession is not necessary unless the Franciscan Superiors (or their delegate) have accepted his resignation, i. e. have dismissed him from the Order.[48]

One who is dismissed from the Order *ipso facto* loses the right to all indulgences and privileges,[49] and in order to become a member a second time, a second novitiate and profession would of necessity be required.[50]

[47] Hilarius Parisiensis, *Liber Tertii Ordinis*, p. 256; The *Rule of Leo* XIII, I, § 3, requires that the scapular and cord must be worn in order to partake of the rights and privileges of the Order and the Sodality; it is but natural that one who freely leaves the Third Order will also cease wearing these, and therefore deprieve himself of the indulgences and privileges. If such a resignation were accepted, it is equal to dismissal from the Order.

[48] Tischler, *Handbuch zur Leitung des Dritten Ordens*, p. 128 f; Beringer, *Die Ablässe*, II, n. 371; *S. C. of Indulgences*, May 27, 1857 (*Decreta Authentica S. C. Indulg.*, n. 379).

[49] *Rule of Leo XIII*, I, § 3; Benedict XIII, Bull, *Paterna Sedis Apostolicae*, Dec. 10, 1725, § 7 (*Bull. Rom.*, XXII, 285-294); can. 692.

[50] The words of the *Rule of Leo XIII*, III, § 4, "* * * *excedere Ordine jubeantur*", and those of canon 696 "*dimmitatur*", "*expugnatur*", "*dimittere*", can be understood in no other manner than that of complete severance from the Order, i. e. that one is no longer a member: therefore in order to become a member a second time, it is logical that the only method by which this can be obtained is by the performance of those actions which are required to become a member—which in the case of the Third Order is brought about by novitiate and profession. One might object by adducing as a parity canon 704 which states that the profession of a Secular Tertiary who has taken religious vows, auto-

A Third Order Sodality is a moral person organically constituted, with its Director and Tertiary officials, and therefor in cases where sufficient reason for dismissal is not openly apparent, it is well that the officials of the Sodality be consulted, particularly in their monthly meeting with the Director as prescribed in the Ceremonial of the Third Order, Article IV.[31]

The dismissal of a *Solitarius* involves some difficulty regarding the required jurisdiction. Practically speaking, this question seldom arises, as Tertiaries with few exceptions belong to Sodalities, and if they do not, there is very little room for observance on the part of the Franciscan Superiors as to whether such Tertiaries are fulfilling their obligations; for the very reason of their isolation from other Tertiaries, the main reason of their dismissal—scandal and consequent laxity in other Tertiaries—becomes obviously insignificant. According to the general principles of jurisdiction it is safe to assume that those who receive isolated Tertiaries into the Third Order with legitimate jurisdiction, also have the right of dismissal, for they thus become their Superiors in so far as they are Tertiaries. It would also seem that a safe norm to follow in this regard would be that such Tertiaries are subject to the Franciscan Superiors in whose Territory they reside,

matically revives when he is released from these religious vows. There is no parity here for a) this is a positive disposition of the law for a particular case; b) canon 704 concerns one who of his own free will leaves the Third Order *only indirectly,* and whose resignation is not necessarily accepted by the Superiors of the Third Order; the opposite is true of a dismissed Tertiary, for he is *rejected* from the Order; therefore in the case of the religious, his profession in the Third Order is *silenced,* rather than *dissolved;* c) in canon 704 there is question of one choosing a *higher* state of life, while a disobedient Tertiary chooses a *lower* state by disobeying the Rules and thus subjecting himself to dismissal.

[31] Cf. canon 697, § 1; below chap. VIII, Art. III, § 4.

according to the principles of domicile contained in canons 91-95.

§ 2. The Inter-relation of the Franciscan Jurisdiction.[52]

Although Pius X expressly forbids any distinction between Tertiaries by reason of their name and origin, namely that all are *Franciscan* Tertiaries, no matter to which Franciscan Family they are subject as Tertiaries,[53] nevertheless in order to avoid confusion, distinctive lines must be drawn regarding the intermingling of the jurisdiction of the various Franciscan Families. The very purpose of the Third Order as expressed in the Rule, demands peace, equanimity and harmony among the brethren. How could this be accomplished if a Friar Minor of one obedience (e. g. Leonine) would be allowed to freely concern himself with the Tertiaries under the care of the Franciscans of another obedience (e. g. Conventual)? on the one side there would be disorder and confusion among the Friars Minor themselves as to who enjoyed the juridical rights toward a certain Sodality; on the part of the Tertiaries the disruption would be still more apparent: to whom would they go for advice and instruction on points of the Rule; who would possess authority of dispensing from obligations of the Rule; whom would they obey as their legitimate Superiors? These difficulties are solved by the following norms:

a) Sodalities which have been erected through the jurisdiction of one Franciscan obedience, cannot be transferred to the care of another obedience without having first obtained the consent of the obedience which erected the Sodal-

[52] I. e. the Friars Minor Leonine, Conventual, Capuchin and Third Order *Regular*.

[53] Brief, *Septimo jam pleno,* Oct. 4, 1909, IX (*A. A. S.*, I [1909], 735).

ity;[54] this of necessity also implies permission of that Franciscan obedience to whose jurisdiction the Sodality wishes to be, or is to be, transferred.

b) A Sodality erected by one obedience, but up to the present directed by another obedience living in the same province or city, is lawfully under the authority of the obedience which erected the Sodality, unless this latter obedience legitimately transferred its right of government to another obedience; in other words, under all circumstances, that obedience which erects a Sodality, *ipso jure* has the right of government, until it legitimately transfers it to another obedience.[55] On this principle if a Guardian of the Conventual obedience who had erected a Sodality, would relinquish that territory, nevertheless another obedience (e. g. Leonine) living in the same place would not be able to assume the reigns of government until it had obtained the consent of the Conventual obedience.

c) Sodalities which have been erected by bishops or priests with legitimate delegation, remain under the authority of that Franciscan Family from which the delegation was legitimately received.[56]

d) Novices who have received the habit from one obedience, may for the sake of their own convenience be professed in a Sodality which is under the jurisdiction of another obedience.[57]

e) A priest who has delegated faculties from one obedience to receive into the Third Order, cannot by this faculty alone, also receive Tertiaries into a Sodality which is under

[54] *S. C. of Religious,* Dec. 6, 1911, ad I (*A. A. S.*, IV [1912], 143).

[55] *Ibidem,* ad II.

[56] Pius X, Brief, *Tertium Franciscalium Ordinem,* Sept. 8, 1912 (*A. A. S.*, IV [1912], 584 f).

[57] *S. C. of Indulgences,* March 4, 1903, ad I (*A. S. S.*, XXXV, 638).

the jurisdiction of another obedience.[58]

f) A Tertiary enjoys the benefit of the Papal blessing and the blessing with plenary indulgence, which are allowed on certain days, even though he has received these blessings from a Director of a Sodality which is under the jurisdiction of an obedience different from his own Sodality.[59] *A fortiori* he may validly receive these blessings from a Director of another Sodality which is under the same jurisdiction as his own proper Sodality.

g) If a pastor or any priest who has been Director of a Sodality under the jurisdiction of one obedience, is transferred to a place and there finds a Sodality of a different obedience, he needs no new faculties to direct this Sodality, but he must inform the canonical Visitor that the two together may provide for the Sodality.[60] The same would be true if a Director were transferred to a place where there is a Sodality under the same obedience as the Sodality he formerly directed.

h) For a just cause Tertiaries may transfer from their own Sodality to another which is under the jurisdiction of a different obedience,[61] and for the same reason they may transfer from one Third Order to another, or from one Sodality to another under the same obedience.[62]

The most common and just reason for these various changes from one Third Order to another, or from one Sodality to another, would be change of residence or a similar motive.

[58] *S. C. of Indulgences,* Jan. 30, 1896, ad IV (*M. E.,* 9, Ser. I, vol. IX, 153).

[59] *Ibidem,* ad III.

[60] *S. C. of Indulgences,* March 4, 1903, ad III (*A. S. S.,* XXXV, 638).

[61] *Ibidem,* ad II; can. 705.

[62] Can. 705.

§ 3. The Institution of Directors for Third Order Sodalities.[63]

Nisi privilegium apostolicum aliud expresse caveat, nominatio moderatoris et cappellani pertinet ad loci Ordinarium * * * in associationibus a religiosis vi apostolici privilegii erectis extra propias ecclesias; in associationibus vero erectis a religiosis in propriis ecclesiis requiritur tantum Ordinarii loci consensus, si a Superiore moderator et cappellanus e clero saeculari eligantur..[64]

The Friars Minor enjoy the right of governing Sodalities of the Franciscan Third Order Secular whether these Sodalities are erected in their own proper Churches or outside of them—

The explicit words *moderator* and *Director* were not used in the papal pronouncements wherein the jurisdiction of the Friars Minor over all Tertiaries was asserted, no matter where their Sodality was located, but their equivalent was used: they were given the apostolic privilege of performing everything toward the Tertiaries which is the right and duty of a Director, in one word, to provide for their spiritual welfare in as far as they are Tertiaries.

The oft-quoted words of Benedict XIII are very clear on this matter:[65]

Lamenting the fact that some Tertiaries had not obeyed the Franciscan Superiors he states that 'the Holy See desires the Tertiaries to be under the care and jurisdiction of the Minister-General and the provincials',[66] and in the same

[63] In this treatise the word *'Director'* is used instead of *'Moderator'* as in can. 698, as this is the common term used for one at the head of a Franciscan Third Order Sodality.

[64] Can. 698, § 1.

[65] Bull, *Paterna Sedis Apostolicae,* Dec. 10, 1725 (*Bull. Rom.*, XXII, 285-294).

[66] "* * * dicti Ordinis saeculares * * * ministri generalis * * * et provincialium * * * curae et jurisdictioni * * * haec Sancta Sedes eos subesse voluit * * *" (§ 5).

paragraph he especially deplores the fact that the ordinaries of the places, 'either at their own instance, or at the instigation of the Tertiaries' (*aut sua sponte, aut ad eorum fratrum Tertiariorum instantiam*), have unlawfully exercised jurisdiction over the Tertiaries; he therefore renews and approves each and every Apostolic constitution which had given any jurisdiction to the Friars Minor over the Tertiaries. But here the pontiff may be said to be speaking only in general terms.

Speaking more specifically, he demands that all Tertiaries (*universis et singuli hujusmodi instituti professoribus*)—therefore those who are members of Sodalities erected outside of Franciscan Churches, as well as those who erected in them—should obey the Minister-General and his secondary Superiors, and even the commissary visitors (*commissarios visitatores*) in all things: 'in all doubts and controversies concerning the Rule and statutes, in fact in all things which pertain to the Order and are not contrary to the Rule', otherwise these Superiors may deprive them of the habit (*cassari atque habitu spoliari possint*), and such disobedient Tertiaries are *ipso facto* deprived of all spiritual favors as well as privileges of the Order. (§ 7.)

In the following paragraph he expressly conceded to the Friars Minor the privilege of establishing Directors outside of Franciscan Churches. The Minister-General is enjoined that through his Secondary Superiors Sodalities of the Third Order shall be established everywhere, Tertiaries shall be received, and to these he shall assign, to the exclusion of all others a 'commissary visitor or confessor, of suitable age and sanctity of life, who shall administer the sacraments, instruct in the Rule, call the meetings, preside at these and all other functions, and cast the deciding vote in the event of a tie.' (§ 8.)"[67]

Not only has this right of the Friars Minor been acknowledged by succeeding pontiffs, but they have also urged that it be put to practical use. Leo XIII, in an audience granted to the four Ministers-General of the First Order and the Third Order Regular, places upon them the obligation of promoting the Third Order through their own priests and visitors, and where there are no religious of the Order, through *delegated* Directors.[68]

[67] Note is to be taken of the words 'commissarium visitatorem'; for this is evidently a *delegation*, and therefore refers not to one who performs this office in a Franciscan Church or convent, but to a place where delegation is required to exercise this authority—therefore in a place outside of Franciscan Churches or convents—for the same pontiff, in speaking of Franciscans providing for the Tertiaries gives this office to the 'secondary Superiors'; thus also the *Statuta Innocentiana* (which were promulgated before the time of Benedict XIII and which he himself approves in this Bull) calls the Guardian the *Ordinary* in his district: therefore he requires no delegation. It should also be noted that in papal documents the word visitor is used promiscuously for both the *canonical* visitor and the Director (or moderator as in canon 696, § 1); hence the office indicated must be determined not by the name used, but rather by his rights and duties as enumerated in the context of the papal documents. Hence from the manifold duties which Benedict XIII places upon this visitor, it is evident that he has reference to the person who today is called Director or moderator, for in the same paragraph of the Bull, immediately following the words cited above, he enumerates the duties of the one who performs the *canonical visitation* in Third Order Sodalities; therefore he has reference to two distinct persons: the Director or moderator, and the visitor. Thus also Pius X uses the words 'praesides seu Visitatores', but from his description of this person and his duties it is clear that he has reference to the Drector.—Brief, *Tertium Franciscalium Ordinem*, Sept. 8, 1912 (*A. A. S.*, IV [1912], 584).

[68] July 7, 1883 (*A. M.*, 110 f; Fleming, *Acta Leonis XIII ad III Ord. Spectantia*, p. 36); cf. the *Ceremonial of the Third Order* approved a short time before this audience by the same pontiff (June 18, 1883), wherein the Director of whom Leo XIII speaks, imposes the habit, receives profession, and presides at the functions of the Sodality.

Pius X is still more explicit on this point, and advocates the spread of the Third Order by saying that 'nothing could be more opportune than that Sodalities are erected not only in Franciscan Churches or convents (coenobia), but also in other places, especially in parish churches whose priests should be delegated as moderators with the advice of the bishop, unless there are reasons to the contrary, *salvo semper jure et officio praelatorum Ordinis Primi'.*[69]

The Franciscan Superiors may therefore delegate Directors outside of their own proper Churches and convents. How far do the rights of the Ordinary of the place reach in the matter of establishing such Directors? Order and the principles of jurisdiction in the Church demand that a priest from one parish cannot, even though he has received the delegation of Director from the Franciscan Superiors, freely invade another parish and there direct a Tertiary Sodality. Therefore canon 696 § 1 provides that when Sodalities are erected outside of Franciscan Churches, the ordinary of the place should appoint the priest who is to be director of the Sodality; this priest in turn shall apply for faculties to direct the Sodality from the Franciscan Superiors. This is in reality what Pius X inculcates in the Brief cited above when he states that upon the advice of the bishop, the care of these Sodalities should be given to the secular clergy of the Church wherein the Sodality is erected. The permission of the bishop is required for the erection of these Tertiary Sodalities (can. 703 § 2; 686 § 3), and therefore it would not be going beyond the meaning of canon 698 § 1, that when a pastor applies for this permission of erection, the ordinary of the place is understood to be giving him permission to Direct the Sodality with the required

[69] Brief, *Tertium Franciscalium Ordinem,* Sept. 8, 1912 (*A. A. S.,* IV [1912], 584 f); this has equal reference to the Third Order Regular—cf. above p. 110 f.

delegation of the Franciscan Superiors. This also has its practical value, for thus the Friars Minor can delegate the pastor, *ratione officii,*[70] so that the next incumbent in office will also be Director without the necessity of recurring to the Franciscan Superiors for delegation.

If the Friars Minor would delegate a priest without consulting the ordinary of the place, his directorship would be valid but illicit, for since they enjoy ordinary jurisdiction, they may freely delegate it to others; besides canon 698 § 1 does not contain an invalidating clause and prescribes no set method of installing in office.

If a Friar Minor, whether by ordinary or delegated authority, is to be Director in a place outside of the Order, he is required to obtain the consent of the ordinary of the place as well as his religious Superior; if he is to be Director in another Church or convent of the Order, he requires the consent of *his* Superior as well as that of the pastor or Superior of the place where he is to be Director; the ordinary of the place has no rights in regard to Friars Minor who are Directors in Franciscan Churches.[71] If, however, a secular priest is to be Director of a Sodality in a Church or convent of the Friars Minor, the consent of the ordinary of the place is required;[72] it does not seem that this consent would be required for a priest who belonged to a community without vows, for although he cannot be called a religious,[73] he nevertheless has his own superiors besides the ordinary of the place.[74] If a religious other than a Friar Minor is to be director in a Church or Convent of the Friars Minor, only the consent of his Superior is required; if in a

[70] Cf. can. 58.
[71] Can. 698, § 1.
[72] *Ibidem.*
[73] Can. 673.
[74] Cf. can. 673-681.

Church or Convent outside of the jurisdiction of the Friars Minor, his religious Superior as well as the ordinary of the place is to be consulted.[75]

In the event that the Friars Minor would recall the delegation of a Director and it would be accepted by him,[76] if they (the Friars Minor) refused to provide for the Tertiaries, there is no reason why the Tertiaries could not have recourse to the Franciscan major Superiors, and this failing, to the S. C. of Religious.[77]

The Ministers-General in the whole world, the provincials in their provinces and the local Superiors in their districts have ordinary jurisdiction to erect and direct Sodalities.[78] Due to the limitation of the territory ordinarily accorded to a local Superior, it is obvious that the delegation to erect and direct Sodalities should generally be sought from the Ministers-General or the provincials.

The ordinary of the place has the right to recall the Directors whom he has the right to appoint,[79] although through this revocation, such Directors would not lose the jurisdiction which has been accorded them by the Friars Minor.[80] The same may be said regarding the other superiors in the various cases cited above.

§ 4. The Discretorium or officials of a Sodality.

One of the privileges arising from the fact that a Third Order Sodality is a moral person, is that its members have juridical rights regarding the government and affairs of the

[75] Can. 698, § 1.
[76] Can. 207, § 1.
[77] Cf. 251, § 1; *A. S. S.*, XXVI, 238-247.
[78] Cf. above chap. VIII, Art. II, § 3.
[79] Can. 698, § 3.
[80] Cf. can. 207, § 1.

Sodality.[81] This authority is therefore vested not only in the Director, but also in the officials of the Sodality chosen by the members to represent the whole, who together with the Director shall convene monthly and decide on affairs of the local organization.[82] Acts decided upon at these meetings without the Director or his delegate presiding have no juridical value.[83] This is evident from the ordinary canonical authority which the Friars Minor or their delegate have the right of exercising over Tertiary Sodalities.

On the other hand it is against the principles of canon law and the juridical concept of the government and organization of a moral person that the Director of a Sodality entirely assume to himself the full authority over the Sodality, especially regarding matters of importance which require deliberation, without giving the board of officials any voice in the matter.[84] In addition to the right of consultation, each of these officials has separate duties. The number of offices that shall be created and filled is best regulated by the needs of each Sodality, depending on the number of Tertiaries and their activities.[85] In the Rule of Leo XIII the general term *'praefecti'* is used for the various officials[86]—which term Mileta explains by designating the various officials comprehended, together with their duties and obligations, such as novice-master, secretary, treasurer, etc.[87] However the rule of necessity as mentioned above, would indicate the safest and most reasonable norm

[81] Can. 101, § 1; 697; 691.
[82] *Ceremonial of the Third Order,* Art. VIII.
[83] *Statuta Innocentiana* ad Cap. XIII.
[84] Cf. Stein, *Tertius Ordo Franciscalis,* p. 68-72; Woywood, "The Director and the Board of Officers", *Third Order Forum,* VI [1927], p. 53-56; Holzapfel, *Die Leitung des Dritten Ordens,* p. 104-124.
[85] *Statuta Innocentiana* ad Cap. XV.
[86] II, §§ 11 and 13.
[87] Mileta, *Enchiridion pro Directoribus Tertii Ordinis,* p. 60-70.

in determining the number of officials and their duties.

There is nothing in the Code or in the Rule of the Third Order forbidding the practice of instituting two bodies of discretorii or officials, that is, one for each sex of the same Sodality; this is rather to be commended than condemned, for it is evident that the office of vigilance over the novices (novice-master, novice-mistress), care of the sick and poor can the better be discharged if the officials are of the same sex as those under their care. This practice is tacitly confirmed by the *Ceremonial of the Third Order,* which states that the same method of procedure is to be followed in the election of Tertiary women and men.[88] But in this event the Tertiaries of both sexes would not be excused from attending the monthly meetings, unless there were two distinct Sodalities: the one for men, the other for women.[89]

The institution of officials: The selection of officials for various offices of a Sodality is a matter which touches upon the welfare of the whole body; hence Leo XIII wisely enacts that the elections are to take place by calling together all the members of the Sodality,[90] that is, by a free election and confirmation by the head of the chapter or gathering, i. e. the Director.[91]

Canon 697 § 2 clearly rules that these elections are to be carried out according to canons 161-182 and according to particular statutes which are not contrary to these canons. Neither is there any reason to depart from this method in

[88] Article IV.

[89] For reasons of diversity of sex and other just causes, separate Sodalities can be erected in the same place.—*S. C. of Indulgences,* March 8, 1905 (*M. E.*, 7, Ser. II, vol. XVII, 204).

[90] "Officia, advocatis ad conventum sodalibus, deferantur * * *" (Rule *of Leo XIII,* III, § 1); that this is an election and not a mere installation of one who has been selected before, is clear from the words of the Ceremonial of the Third Order, Art. V.

[91] Can. 162; 174; 177.

conferring the offices of the Sodality. Some would mitigate the procedure of the Code in this regard, using the argument that since a Third Order Sodality is only an association of the laity, not all the laws of the Code are to be strictly observed as in solemn canonical elections, thus distinguishing between elections *majoris et minoris momenti.*[92] But in the present case this argument seems to have little weight for canon law expressly and clearly states that these elections are to take place according to canons 161-182, and according to statutes which are not opposed to it.[93] Neither can it be said that the Code does not intend this method for the laity as well as the clergy, for the canons bearing on election indicate that it is for both laity and clergy.[94] Therefore since Canon law ordains a specific method of installing in office, there seems to be no room for distinction.[95]

Besides, elections of lay people which are carried out according to the norms of canon law do not imply such a great difficulty of procedure: even according to the *Rule of Leo XIII,* all the members of the Sodality must be called in order that the elections may take place.[96] Why then should there be such great difficulty in following out the remainder of the prescriptions of common law? Then, too,

[92] Thus, Stein, *Tertius Ordo Franciscalis,* p. 70 f, uses these arguments by referring to elections of major and minor moment, as brought out by the *S. C. of Bishops and Regulars* in 1865 (*A. S. S.*, I, 153-163), and in 1867 (*o. c.*, 234-238); he also refers to Reiffenstuel, Tom. I, tit. 6, *de elec.*, 112 for this distinction.

[93] Can. 697, § 2.

[94] Cf. can. 172, §2.

[95] Cocchi, *Commentarium,* IV, n. 181; Vermeersch-Creusen, *Epitome,* I, n. 789; Augustine, *A Commentary,* III, p. 438; Ferreres, *Institutiones Canonicae,* I, n. 969; Chelodi, *Jus de Personis,* n. 299, do not attempt to mitigate this method of election in any manner; they simply state that the common law of canons 161-182 and particular statutes not opposed to it, must be observed.

[96] *Rule,* III, § 1.

canon 697 permits the use of statutes which are not contrary to the common law. Thus canon 162 § 1 allows custom or statute to be used in calling together the electors. It is a simple matter to summon the Tertiaries to the election at the monthly meeting prescribed in the Ceremonial, Art. I, and in this manner there is very little danger of a third of the members being neglected as to render the election invalid.[97] If these monthly meetings are held regularly and the Tertiaries are instructed to attend these (which they will if they are not neglectful), there is no reason why one of these conferences cannot be used to summon them to the triennial (Cf. Rule, III § 1) election; for this reason if a third were absent it cannot be said that they were neglected in the sense of canon 162 § 3; rather it is through their own neglect that they were absent, and it is practically impossible that a third of the members of the Sodality will have a *legitimate* excuse for absence;[98] the defect of summons does not invalidate the election, provided those who were neglected were present.[99] The voting must be secret under pain of invalidity;[100] consequently even particular statute cannot validly allow votes to be cast in any other manner. On either the first or second ballot, he is considered elected who has received more than half of the votes validly cast; on the third ballot a relative majority is sufficient, that is, he is elected who has received the greatest number of votes among those who were favored in any way; if the votes are equal on this ballot, the head of the

[97] Can. 162, § 3.

[98] It is not necessary that all the Tertiaries be present at the election: provided the summons is legitimately made, the right of election devolves upon those who answer the summons by attending the election. (Can. 163.)

[99] Can. 162, §4.

[100] Can. 169, § 1, 2°.

chapter or gathering may cast the deciding vote;[101] if he declines to do this, he is considered elected who is senior in orders,[102] profession, or age among those who have received an equal number of votes on the third ballot.[103] Confirmation of the one who is elected is made by the head of the chapter or gathering; this cannot be denied if the one elected is suitable for the office and the election had been legitimately conducted.[104]

An example of a diversion from the ordinary canonical method is that given in canon 172 § 1 wherein the full right of election is given by the electing Tertiaries to one or more of the electors, or to one who is extraneous to those who are electing; this authority must be given unanimously and in writing.[105] This mode of procedure in conducting elec-

[101] Can. 101, § 1, 1°; Benedict XIII, *Paterna Sedis Apostolicae,* Dec. 10, 1725, § 8 (*Bull. Rom.,* XXII, 285-294), mentions of the Director: "duplex etiam in paritate suffragium ferat;" Woywood, "The Director and the Board of Officers", *Third Order Forum,* VI [1927], p. 54, denies to the president of the chapter the right to cast a vote, quoting canon 715 as an argument. While it is true that canon 697, § 1, after stating that associations legitimately erected have the right of electing officers, at the end adds the words: "*firmo praescripto can. 715*", it by no means implies thereby that canon 715 must be observed in the elections of *all* associations; 'firmo praescripto' simply means that canon 715 must be observed, that is, all associations should conduct their elections according to common law, while in the elections of officials for confraternities, the additional prescriptions of canon 715 are binding. Did canon 697 § 1 use the words '*ad normam can. 715*', then one would have to admit that this latter would be common law for elections in all associations; but the words '*firmo praescripto can. 715*' indicate that this canon must be observed in those things to which it has reference, namely in the elections of officials for *confraternities* alone. Therefore canon 715 has no reference to the elections of officials for Third Order Sodalities, for the Third Order is not a confraternity.

[102] Cf. can. 106, 3°.

[103] Cf. can. 174; 101, § 1, 1°.

[104] Can. 177, § 2.

[105] Can. 172-173.

tions may be employed by any association in which there is no law to the contrary,[106] and since there is nothing in the Rule of the Third Order forbidding it, this method may be *favored* in the statutes; this act of giving one or more persons the full right of selecting for office is known as a *compromise.*[107]

Under no consideration may the practice be allowed of Directors of Sodalities choosing for office without consulting the members of the Sodality.[108] Such procedure is evidently invalid for the Director would be assuming to himself a right which was never given to him;[109] it is entirely opposed to the juridical concept of a moral person with the inherent right of its members to elect their officials,[110] and this practice has been reprimanded by the Holy See: in a dispute between a Tertiary Sodality and the Franciscan Superiors, the S. C. of the Council was asked whether these offices should be filled by the Superiors alone, or ac-

[106] Can. 172, § 1.

[107] Can. 172, § 1. The word *favored* is used because this method could not safely be embodied in the statutes as a set of mode of procedure, for the reason that those who have the right of electing must unanimously consent to this usage—which consent must be given at each election, for it would be no more than gratuitous to assert that the same Tertiaries who take part in one election, will also take part in the next, and will consent to this compromise; Cf. Chelodi, *Jus de Personis*, n. 139, c; only a sketch of an election is given here, and therefore statutes and the remainder of the canons bearing on election must necessarily be consulted regarding the other requirements for election, as well as the necessary qualifications of the one who is elected and the electors. This latter consideration, however, will cause little difficulty if the Director is vigilant regarding the reception and rejection of undesirable Tertiaries as has been outlined above.—cf. above chap. VIII, Art. III, § 1.

[108] Thus Cerri, *Il Terz' Ordine Francescano*, p. 77, while favoring a free election, is of the opinion that absolutely speaking, offices can be conferred by the Director alone.

[109] *Rule of Leo XIII*, III, § 1; can. 697.

[110] *Ibidem;* can. 101.

cording to the statutes of the Third Order, i. e. by a free election; the Congregation replied that the latter method must be used.[111]

The practice of the Director naming certain individual Tertiaries as being suitable for certain offices is not contrary to the Code, provided that entire freedom is allowed to the electors to choose either those who were mentioned or others. In fact this is to be commended if there is danger that the electors have insufficient knowledge of the qualities and capabilities of the various members of the Sodality.

The authority of the officials is to be considered as domestic, rather than dominative, and subject to the Superior or Director of the Sodality.[112] On the other hand the Director would be derogating from the juridical rights which a Sodality enjoys as a moral person were he to arrogate to himself entirely the complete government. Hence in affairs of greater moment the officials are not to be ignored, e. g. regarding the reception and expulsion of members. It is evidently with this thought in view that the *Ceremonial of the Third Order* prescribes a monthly meeting of the Director with the officials of the Sodality.[113]

§ 5. The Administration of the Goods of a Tertiary Sodality.

Unless expressly forbidden to the contrary, all associations legitimately erected may possess and administer temporal goods.[114] From the very beginning, the Rule of the Third Order, far from forbidding the possession of tem-

[111] Aug. 25, 1893, ad III (*A. S. S.*, XXVI, 485-498).
[112] Stein, *Tertius Ordo Franciscalis*, p. 71.
[113] Article IV. In the following pages the rights of the officials in respect to the administration of the goods of a Sodality will be outlined.
[114] Can. 691, § 1.

poral goods, has rather encouraged it, especially for the care of the sick and the poor as will be presently shown. The present *Rule of Leo XIII* explicitly demands the administration of temporal goods when it specifies that the sick shall be cared for in a charitable manner from the contributions of the members of the Sodality.[115] Necessarily connected with the possession of temporal goods is the question regarding whose competence and right it is to administer them.

In a Sodality of the Third Order Secular of St. Francis, the officials or Discretorium alone have the right of administering its properties.

The following three-fold proof is offered: a) that this right has always resided in the Tertiary officials from the beginning of the Order; b) that it was never legitimately transferred to the Franciscan Superiors; c) that present canon law gives this right to the Tertiary officials.

A) *This right has always resided in the officials of the Sodality.* The first Rule of the Order makes provision that the ministers, i. e. the officials, with the consent of the brethren, shall elect two other officials and a treasurer (massarius) who are to provide for the Tertiaries and the poor.[116] The Rule of 1289 by Nicholas IV mentions that at divine services a collection should be taken up by the treasurer, and with the consent of the officials, should be utilized by him to alleviate the sufferings of the poor as well as the sick, and to defray funeral expenses.[117] The officials shall visit the sick weekly in order to provide for their neces-

[115] *Rule,* II, §§ 12 and 13.

[116] "Ministri cum consilio suorum fratrum post annum eligant duos alios ministros et fidelem massarium qui necessitati fratrum et sororum et aliorum pauperum provideat et nuntios qui dicta factaque fraternitatis de mandato eorum nuntiet." (XII, 6.)

[117] Chap. XIII.

sities from the common funds (de bonis communibus ministrando).[118]

In the *Statuta Innocentiana* the care of all moneys which may come to the Sodality is to be placed in the hands of one of the officials called a '*Syndicus*' (procurator), and is to be expended by him, subject to the wishes of the minister.[119]

The same tenor is expressed in statutes and chapters of individual places; thus the Chapter of Tertiaries held at Bologna (1289) decreed that no Tertiary shall be allowed to collect any temporal goods without the permission of the ministers (officials);[120] the Statutes of the Congregation of Brescia (13th century) state that the Minister (chief official) shall, after his term has expired, turn over the goods of the community to his successor and the officials (ministro sequenti et officialibus), and render a strict account of these goods.[121]

Benedict XIII speaks of the deputies and officials as ad-

[118] Chap. XIV.

[119] Ad Cap. XV, s. v. *Officium Syndici;* the minister is the chief official of the Sodality and himself a Tertiary. By the minister is not meant the Franciscan Superior, for the same chapter (s. v. *Officium discretorum*) enumerates the authority of a Sodality as follows: "* * * in congregatione [Sodality according to the present canonical term] Guardiani, Ministri, Visitatoris, Discretorum, et Secretarii consistat gubernium totius Ordinis, * * *." And again the same chapter (s v. Officium Ministri)—"Notandum vero: si minister sit *saecularis, Coadjutorem* debere esse *sacerdotem;* et e contra si Minister fuerit *sacerdos,* Coadjutor debet esse *saecularis.*" Therefore the minister is not the Franciscan Superior. The italics in this quotation are in the Statutes.

[120] *A. F. H.*, II, p. 69 f, § 11.

[121] *A. F. H.*, I, p. 551, n. XXI; that this minister is not a Friar Minor is also apparent from these statutes wherein the minister is enjoined to call a Friar Minor in case of discordance among the brethren. (n. X.)

ministering the funds of the Tertiary Sodality,[122] while Leo XIII in his Rule demands that the praefecti (officials) fulfill their office of charity toward the sick and care for them in a temporary manner, i. e. provide them with temporal necessities.[123]

B) *This right which the officials enjoyed from the very beginning of the Order was never transferred to the Franciscan Superiors.* In the beginning of the existence of the Third Order, The Friars Minor had little or nothing to do with its government ex jure, as can be surmised from the first Rule of the Order which does not commemorate the Franciscans in any way.[124]

Gradually through papal decree and statute the Friars Minor assumed complete authority over the Tertiaries; however, this authority, although ordinary, was spiritual alone, i. e. it never extended itself to the temporal goods of a Sodality. At its inception the entire government, even including the office of visitation, was vested in the Tertiaries themselves, or by someone appointed by them who in many cases was a Friar Minor;[125] in 1234 this latter office was given to the ordinary of the place in order to free the Tertiaries from the molestations of the civil authorities.[126]

The first instance of any canonical authority being conceded to the Friars Minor was in the year 1247 when Innocent IV authorized them to perform the office of visitation,

[122] Benedict XIII, Bull, *Paterna Sedis Apostolicae,* Dec. 10, 1725, § 8 (*Bull. Rom.,* XXII, 285-294).

[123] *Rule of Leo XIII,* II, §§ 12 and 13.

[124] Cf. the *Regula Antiqua* in the appendix; the thirteenth chapter, which makes mention of the Friars Minor, was inserted around 1247 as has already been mentioned and will shortly be noted.

[125] The testimony of Bernard of Besse implies this—cf. "Liber de Laudibus", *Analecta Franciscana,* III, p. 686.

[126] Bull, *Ut cum majori,* Nov. 21, 1234 (*Bull. Franc.,* I, n. 149, p. 142 f).

to instruct in the Rule, to correct and reform the Tertiaries 'both in head and members.'[127] The Rule of Nicholas IV (1289) counsels that the Friars Minor visit and reform the Tertiary Congregations,[128] while the Statutes of the Congregation of Brescia (13th century) enjoin the Minister of the Tertiary Congregation to call a Friar Minor in case of discordance among the brethren.[129]

John XXII describes the dependence of the Tertiaries as being *'sub cura et doctrina Fratrum Minorum.'*[130] To garb with the habit, receive profession, perform the office of visitation and to appoint a confessor is the extent of the jurisdiction of the Friars Minor over the Tertiaries as mentioned by Sixtus IV.[131]

The foregoing decrees are more or less of a negative character; but the words of Benedict XIII treat the question under consideration in a positive manner. After declaring the authority of the Friars Minor to consist in erecting Tertiary Congregations (Sodalities), receiving profession, instructing in the Rule, settling controversies, and administering to the Tertiaries in general, he gives them authority through the canonical visitor appointed by them, to examine whether the temporal goods have been properly administered, but he expressly *forbids* them to administer the same *as this is the duty of the officials of the Sodality.*[132]

[127] Bull, *Vota devotorum,* June 13, 1247 (*Bull. Franc.,* I, n. 210, p. 464); this decree was embodied in the Regula Antiqua at that time under XIII, 5-6.

[128] Chap. XVI.

[129] *A. F. H.,* I, p. 549, n. X.

[130] *Orbis Seraphicus,* II, 793 f.

[131] Bull, *Romani Pontificis,* Dec. 15, 1471 (*o. c.,* 893-895).

[132] "Visitator * * * libròs et rationes redituum ac bonorum ipsarum congregationum examinare et recognoscere poterit, *quin in eorum administratione aut eleemosynarum receptione vel distributione se ingerant,* sed tantum an videlicet deputati et officiales piis operibus ac legatis, oneribusque praefatae congregationi injunctis et impositis,

All other decrees of the Holy See in granting authority over the secular Tertiaries to the Friars Minor, always limit themselves to the spiritual subjection of the Tertiaries to them.[123]

debitis modo et forma et opportuno tempore satisfaciant. * * * "—Bull, *Paterna Sedis Apostolicae,* Dec. 10, 1725, § 8 (*Bull. Rom.*, XXII, 285-294).

[123] Clement X gave authority to the Capuchins and the Third Order Regular to confer the habit and to govern the Third Order according to previous legislation (*Sollicitudo Pastoralis,* Feb. 20, 1675 (*Bull. Rom.*, XVIII, 540-542); the following is a decree of the S. C. of Bishops and Regulars, June 18, 1717, in reference to the jurisdiction of the *Patres Reformati* over the Tertiaries: "An Tertiarii sint subjecti gubernio spirituali Patrum Reformatorum in casu?" Response, "Affirmative in cernentibus *spiritualia* in ecclesia S. Antonii." (*Fontes,* n. 1834); "erigere, instutuere et fundare Tertium Ordinem, * * * atque hujusmodi Tertii Ordinis professoribus * * * scapulare sive habitum cum cingulo conferre, in rebus spiritualibus dirigere, in tertia Regula beati Francisci observanda privatim et publice docere et instruere', is the extent of the jurisdiction of the Friars Minor Capuchin as given by Benedict XIII in the Bull, *Ratio Apostolici ministerii,* June 23, 1726, and by Clement XII in the Bull, *Apostolicae servitutis,* July 23, 1735 (*Bull. Rom.*, XXII, 369, § 3, and XXIV, 61, § 1, respectively); the *Rule of Leo XIII* gives authority only in those things which are spiritual (cf. Rule, chap. III); the various Bulls of Benedict XIII, Clement XII and Benedict XIV (Bull, *Laudabile,* Aug. 2, 1745—*Bull. Rom. Continuatio,* I, 547-550) have definitely settled the question of the jurisdiction of the Friars Minor over the Secular Tertiaries; hence there are no later papal decrees which treat this *ex professo.* However, there are many other more recent papal pronouncements which treat of the jurisdiction of the Friars Minor, but in none of these will the reader discover any connections which are other than spiritual: cf. Leo XIII, Encyclical, *Auspicato,* Sept. 7, 1882 (*A. S. S.*, XV, 145-153); Leo XIII, Const., *Misericors Dei Filius,* May 30, 1883 (*Fontes,* n. 588), the words of Leo XIII in an audience granted to the four Ministers-General of the Friars Minor and the Third Order Regular, July 7, 1883 (*A. M.*, II, 111); Pius X, Brief, *Sodalium e Tertio Ordine,* May 5, 1909 (*A. M.*, XXVIII, 174-176); Pius X, Brief, *Septimo jam pleno,* Oct. 4, 1909 (*A. A. S.*, I [1909], 725-739); Pius X, Brief, *Tertium Franciscalium Ordinem,* Sept. 8, 1912 (*A. A. S.*, IV [1912], 582-586); Pius X, Brief, *Recte vos,* Apr. 25, 1909 (*A. A. S.*, I [1909], 485-487); Benedict XV, Brief, *Sacra Propediem,* Jan. 6, 1921 (*A. A. S.*, XIII

Arguing therefore from the principle of canon 4 that the administration of the goods of a Sodality is a right which was always exercised by the officials of a Sodality and was never taken from them legitimately, this right must be upheld to the exclusion of others.

C) *Canon law gives the Tertiary officials the right of administering the goods of a Sodality.* All associations legitimately erected may possess as well as administer properties,[134] and if the association is a moral person, that person itself is the subject of its temporalities,[135] which necessarily comes under the heading of ecclesiastical goods.[136] Since a moral person is equal to a minor,[137] it is necessary that it act through individuals as administrators, whom the members of a moral person have the right to elect.[138] These are known by the common term of officials in Sodalities of the Third Order Secular.

Consequently the Franciscan Superior or his delegate as head of a local Sodality, has no direct part in the administration of its funds but nevertheless has the right of vigilance regarding their disposal; this office of vigilance is also to be exercised at the time of the canonical visitation.[139]

The following points are to be observed regarding the goods of a Sodality: a) alms may be collected and used for

[1921], 33-41); Benedict XV, Brief, *Terti Ordinis a poenitentia,* Feb. 20, 1921 (*A. A. S.,* XIII [1921], 130 f); Pius XI, Const., *Rite expiatis,* Apr. 30, 1926 (*A. A. S.,* XVIII [1926], 153-175).

[134] Can. 691, § 1.

[135] Can. 1499, § 2; "Subjectum bonorum ad associationes juridica persona gaudentes, residet in ipsa persona morali."—Cocchi, *Commentarium,* IV, n. 177.

[136] Can. 1497, § 1.

[137] Can. 100, § 3.

[138] Can. 697, § 1; 1495, § 2.

[139] Benedict XIII, Bull, *Paterna Sedis Apostolicae,* Dec. 10, 1725, § 8, (*Bull. Rom.,* XXII, 285-294).

pious purposes, but the will of the donors must be complied with;[140] b) the permission of the ordinary of the place where the Sodality is erected must be obtained,[141] and if alms are to be collected outside of the diocese where the Sodality is situated, the permission of the ordinaries of both places must be obtained in writing;[142] c) although the temporal goods of a Third Order Sodality are subject by papal decree to the vigilance of the Friars Minor,[143] nevertheless the ordinary of the place has the right to demand an annual account of their disposal.[144] d) on the contrary, donations prescribed by the Rule[145] which are to be made by the Tertiaries themselves for a common fund to be used for the poor and sick members, refer to the *internal discipline* of the Sodality, concerning which the ordinary of the place has no right of vigilance.[146] e) the administrators of Tertiary property cannot take part in court procedure concerning the same without the permission of the ordinary of the place.[147]

§ 6. The Canonical Visitation.

Too much stress cannot be placed on the importance of this office, for just as bishops are required canonically to visit the various institutions of their dioceses in order to correct abuses which may have crept in, and to promote

[140] Can. 691, § 2.

[141] Can. 691, § 3.

[142] Can. 691, § 4.

[143] Benedict XIII, Bull, *Paterna Sedis Apostolicae*, Dec. 10, 1725, § 8 (*Bull. Rom.*, XXII, 285-294).

[144] Can. 691, §§ 1 and 5; 1525.

[145] *Rule of Leo XIII*, II, § 12.

[146] Can. 690, § 2; this refers equally as well to Sodalities erected outside of Franciscan churches and convents, for the Friars Minor have the right of governing these Sodalities in regard to their internal affairs, as has been stated above in § 3 of this Article.

[147] Can. 1526; Vermeersch-Creusen, *Epitome*, II, n. 848.

discipline,[148] so also are the Franciscan Superiors required to keep vigil over the various Tertiary Sodalities under their jurisdiction—which vigil is best observed by the canonical visitation prescribed by Leo XIII.[149]

"*Visitatores* ex Primo Franciscalium Ordine, vel Ordine Tertio Regulari legantur, quos custodes seu *Guardiani,* si id rogati fuerint, designabunt. *Visitatoris* munere laicis viris interdictum esto."[150]

The Rule indicates that the Minister-General or the Provincial—which would be more practical—should designate the visitor who would thus enjoy faculties to visit all Sodalities which have been erected under his jurisdiction. The words of the Rule quoted above, in speaking of the Guardian designating the visitor, adds this significant clause: *si id rogati fuerint;* but the same Rule demands that this visitation should be made yearly,[151] and therefore it is not a matter of choice on the part of the Guardian. Ordinarily then, the Visitor should be designated by the Provincial, extraordinarily by the Guardian. This solution also has its practical value: visitation primarily tends toward the correction of abuses and the promotion of harmony both between the Tertiaries themselves, as also between the Tertiaries and their Director—an office which of its nature requires tact and experience which would hardly be acquired by the visitation of one or two Sodalities of a Guardianship. This view is further strengthened by the fact that Leo XIII, although prescribing annual visitation, adds that if necessity demands, it can be made more often.[152] Therefore ordinarily the visitor is the dele-

[148] Can. 343; 346.
[149] *Rule of Leo XIII,* III, § 2.
[150] *Ibidem,* § 3; the italics belong to the Rule.
[151] *Ibidem,* § 2—*in singulos annos.*
[152] *Ibidem*—"eoque crebrius, si res postulaverit".

gate of the provincial, and if necessity demands, inter-annual visitation may be instituted by the Guardian, *si id rogati fuerint,* i. e. if the Director or the officials of the Sodality deem it expedient and request the Guardian to appoint an extraordinary visitor.[153]

The visitors are to be chosen from among the Friars Minor,[154] and rightly so: for since the Third Order is under their authority, it is entirely in conformity with the principles of jurisdiction that visitation, which is an essential part of the government of any ecclesiastical institution, should be made by those who enjoy that authority. However, due to the fact that Leo XIII positively excludes only lay persons from this office,[155] there is no reason to suppose that a secular priest or another religious priest could not be delegated, especially in isolated places where a Franciscan priest could not easily be obtained; this necessarily postulates a knowledge of the principles and purpose of the Third Order on the part of a priest thus delegated; otherwise the very purpose of the visitation would be frustrated. Prudence, as well as the welfare of the Tertiaries and their local organization demand that a priest should not be Director and visitor of the same Sodality.

The office of visitation is described in the following words by the *Rule of Leo XIII*: "Curator qui *Visitator* audit, diligenter quaerat, satisne salvae leges. Ejust rei ergo, sodalitiorum sedes in singulos annos, eoque crebrius, si res postulaverit, pro potestate circumeat, coetumque habeat, Praefectis[156] sodalibusque universis adesse jussis. Si quem

[153] The *Constitutiones O. M. Conv.*, Cap. XI, Tit. III, n. 11 urge the provincial also to visit the Tertiary Sodalities at the time of his annual visitation of the religious of the First Order.

[154] *Rule of Leo XIII*, III, § 3.

[155] *Ibidem*—"Visitatoris munere laicis interdictum esta".

[156] I. e. officials.

Visitator ad officium monendo jubendo revocarit, sive quid, salutaris poenae nomine, in quemquam decreverit, hic modeste accipiat, idemque luere ne abnuat."[157]

His duty being therefore to inquire as to whether the Rules of the Third Order and the statutes of the local organization are observed; for non-observance he may give salutary punishment; he may also dispense from prescriptions of the Rule in individual cases;[158] he is also to inquire regarding the administration of the funds of the Sodality by its officials.[159]

From the words of the Rule it is evident that the office of visitation is not to be taken lightly, and either neglected or fulfilled at the whim of the Franciscan Superiors; it is to be made yearly and more often if the occasion requires. In this it is also to be remembered that since a Sodality of the Third Order is a moral person, its officials may demand visitation if the Friars Minor are neglectful in this regard, and especially so, because this is one of the chief Rules of the Order. That annual visitation is a duty which devolves upon the Franciscan Superiors even in isolated places is also apparent from the *Statuta Innocentiana.*[160]

The Ordinary of the place regarding visitation. The ordinary of the place has no right of visitation or vigilance in regard to the Rule and internal discipline of Tertiary So-

[157] III, § 2; the italics are in the Rule.

[158] *Ibidem;* § 6.

[159] Benedict XIII, Bull, *Paterna Sedis Apostolicae,* Dec. 10, 1725, § 8 (*Bull. Rom.*, XXII, 285-294).

[160] "Itaque in pagis poterunt fratres, et sorores sollicitare, ut aliquis sacerdos petat a p. Guardiano suam authoritatem, in ordine ad illis assistendum, sicut assistit Visitator religiosus in Civitatibus ubi sunt Conventus. Poterunt similiter facere suas Congregationes, et electiones officiorum. *Nihilominus ad Visitatorem Regularem pertinet semper singulis annis visitare fraternitates Tertii Ordinis,* quae fuerint per totam Guardianiam, si ipse Guardianus nolit facere." (ad Cap. XVI).

dalities, no matter whether they have been erected in the churches of the Friars Minor,[161] or in other places with the delegation of the Franciscan Superiors.[162] He has the right of visitation or of demanding an annual account of the administration of the goods of a Sodality,[163] not however those funds which are collected from the Tertiaries themselves through the obligation of the Rule, as this refers to the internal discipline of a Sodality. If the Tertiaries are assigned a separate chapel in a church of the Friars Minor, the ordinary of the place may visit in regard to the upkeep of its altar, i. e. in those things which entail the administration of funds.[164] He has the right of examining the books regarding the obligations of Masses which by chance the Tertiaries may have.[165] If a Tertiary Sodality is erected in an oratory which belongs to them, this oratory not being exempt, is subject to the visitation of the ordinary of the place in the same manner as other non-exempt institutions of the diocese.[166] The Sacred Consistorial Congregation in its *Ordo Servandus in relatione de statu ecclesiarum,* places upon the ordinary of the place the obligation of ascertain-

[161] Can. 690, § 2; *S. C. of Indulgences,* Jan. 31, 1893, ad III (*A. S. S.,* XXV, 506-509).

[162] These latter Sodalities enjoy the apostolic privilege of which can. 690, § 1, speaks: Benedict XIII, Bull, *Paterna Sedis Apostolicae,* § 8 (*Bull. Rom.,* XXII, 285-294); Cf. *Causa Sypontina,* decided by the *S. C. of Bishops and Regulars,* March 10, 1893 (*A. S. S.,* XXVI, 238-247); this is evident from the fact that it has been proven that the Friars Minor have full rights regarding the discipline and spiritual care of Sodalities no matter where they have been erected.—cf. above § 3 of this article.

[163] Can. 691, § 5; 1525; *Concil. Trident.,* Sess. XXII de reformat., cap. 8-9.

[164] *S. C. of the Council,* June 23, 1719 (Benedict XIV, *Institutiones Ecclesiasticae,* CV, LXXXVII); *Concil. Trident,* l. c.

[165] Piat, *Praelectiones Juris Regularis,* II, Q 78.

[166] Can. 344, § 1.

ing the existence of Tertiaries in the diocese; whether they give a good example to the other faithful; he is also to exercise vigilance as to whether those who are notoriously addicted to a heretical sect are received into the Third Order, and if so, what means are taken to avoid this evil.[167]

§ 7. Summary of the Rights of Franciscan Superiors toward Sodalities.[168]

The Ministers-General in the whole world, the Provincial and local Superiors in their respective territories, to the exclusion of others, enjoy the following rights and privileges which may be exercised either through themselves or others:[169]

a) To erect Sodalities after having received the written consent of the ordinary of the place; to invest with the habit and receive the profession of novices after having received the vote of the officials of the Sodality, although this latter is certainly not necessary for the validity of these acts. b) The very nature of their office demands that they instruct the novices and Tertiaries in the Rule of the Order and its obligations. c) To call the various meetings prescribed in the Ceremonial,[170] and preside over them,

[167] Dec. 31, 1909, nn. 134 f (*A. A. S.*, II [1910], 32).

[168] Many of these points have already been thoroughly treated; hence proofs will only be adduced for those which have not been mentioned before.

[169] Can. 199, § 1.

[170] *The Rule of Leo XIII*, II, § 11, states that the prefect shall call these meetings; the term 'prefect', when applied to the Franciscan Superiors is usually prefixed with the word 'ordinarius' (cf. *Rule*, III, § 6); it would seem therefore that this calling of the various gatherings is the office of one of the lay officials of the Sodality. The meaning of the term therefore is not fully clear, but in view of the fact that Benedict XIII (Bull, *Paterna Sedis Apostolicae*, Dec. 10, 1725, § 8—*Bull. Rom.*, XXII, 285-294) expressly gave this authority to the Fran-

as well as over the monthly meetings of the officials; they also preside at the elections of officials of the Sodality, and as head of the chapter, confirm the elections. d) To correct delinquents for transgressions against the Rule, and after a third unheeded admonition, to expel them from the Order. e) To dispense from prescriptions of the Rule in individual cases for a just and grave cause: this authority comprehends dispensations from fasts, prayers and attendance at monthly meetings as prescribed in chapter III of the Rule; commuting in *particular* cases, the wearing of the scapular into a medal, although a *general* commutation is forbidden.[171] They cannot dispense with the period of the novitiate either in whole or in part, except in danger of death. f) To convoke conventions of the Tertiaries and preside at them according to the following norms: if from a district, the local Superior; if from a province, the Provincial; if from many provinces, the Minister-General. The Superiors of the Third Order Regular are excluded by positive law from this privilege.[172] g) To perform the canonical visitation. h) The Franciscan Superiors have the right to impart the papal blessing, and the blessing with plenary indulgence.[173]

ciscan Superiors, until it is expressly proven otherwise, there is no reason to digress from this practice. Certainly these meetings cannot be called without the authority of the Director.—cf. *S. C. of Indulgences*, Jan. 30, 1896, ad VI (*M. E.*, 9, Ser. I, vol. IX, 153).

[171] *Rule*, III, § 6; I, § 3; *S. C. of Religious*, March 25, 1922 (*A. A. S.*, XIV [1922], 353 f).

[172] "Religiosi dumtaxat ex Ordine Primo coetus seu conventus sodalium Ordinis Tertii cogant iisdemque praesideant; si sodales a *districtu* coeant, coenobii custos seu *Guardianus;* si e provincia, provincialis Minister; si e pluribus provinciis, Ordinis Minister generalis."—Pius X, Brief, *Tertium Franciscalium Ordinem*, Sept. 8, 1912 (*A. A. S.*, IV [1912], 585, I); the italics are in the Brief.

[173] The various phases of these blessings will be explained later.

CHAPTER IX

Privileges and Indulgences of the Franciscan Third Order Secular.

Article I.

The Right of Precedence.

Sodalities of the Third Order Secular of St. Francis enjoy precedence over all lay associations, when they proceed collegiately under the cross or banner proper to the Sodality.[1] This privilege also extends to processions of the Blessed Sacrament in which the confraternity of the Blessed Sacrament takes part.[2]

The right of precedence depends on their observance of proceeding collegiately with the cross or other proper insignia, and on their being clothed with the full habit of the Order, i. e. a garment comprehended in the Italian word *sacco;*[3] that the word *sacco* has reference to the total garment or habit is clear from another decision of the S. C. of Rites which states that this *sacco* is an entire garment

[1] Can. 701; 706; *S. C. of Rites*, May 28, 1886; July 4, 1887; March 27, 1893; March 1, 1894; March 27, 1897; Nov. 30, 1897; Feb. 18, 1899; Nov. 10, 1905 (*Decreta Authentica S. C. R.*, nn. 3664, 3678, 3795, 3819, 3951, 3968, 4012, 4173, respectively).

[2] *Ibidem;* cf. Ferreres, *Le Confraternite*, n. 444.

[3] "* * * tunc sollumodo habere jus preacedentiae in Processionibus, cum iidem collegialiter incedunt sub propria cruce ac veste uniformi induti, vulgo *sacco*."—*S. C. of Bishops and Regulars*, Apr. 6, 1900 (*Fontes*, n. 2038); cf. can. 706.

(vestem integram vulgo saccum);[4] surely the small scapular and cord which is ordinarily worn by the Tertiaries[5] would not be comprehended in this description. Hence if the Tertiaries do not proceed collegiately or do not wear the habit, they do not enjoy right of precedence; therefore since they are obliged to proceed collegiately it is evident that this right does not belong to the Tertiaries as *individuals,* but rather as a body and consequently it is necessary that the Sodality be canonically erected as will shortly be seen.

What if neither the Tertiaries nor the members of other lay associations in procession wear the full garment? In this event the Tertiaries nevertheless enjoy the right of precedence, but they are exhorted to wear the full habit in procession.[6]

Franciscan Tertiaries may also march in procession with the Friars Minor under the cross of the latter.[7]

Among Sodalities of the same or a different Order, the right of precedence is enjoyed by that Sodality which is in quasi-possession of the same,[8] and if this is not clear, by that Sodality which was first canonically erected in the place.[9] In the event of controversy, the ordinary of the place decides questions of precedence;[10] his consent is also required if the Tertiaries wish to wear a special garb. Ter-

[4] Nov. 10, 1905 ad I (*Decreta Authentica S. C. R.*, n. 4173).

[5] Cf. *Rule of Leo XIII*, I, § 3.

[6] *S. C. of Rites*, Nov. 10, 1905, ad I (*Decreta Authentica S. C. R.*, n. 4173).

[7] Benedict XIII, Bull, *Paterna Sedis Apostolicae*, Dec. 10, 1725, § 9 (*Bull. Rom.*, XXII, 285-294); *S. C. of Bishops and Regulars*, Aug. 25, 1893, ad II (*A. S. S.*, XXVI, 497 f).

[8] Can. 106, 5°.

[9] *Ibidem; S. C. of Rites*, March 1, 1894 (*Decreta Authentica S. C. R.*, n. 3819).

[10] Can. 106, 6°.

tiaries may also take part in public processions, funerals, etc., without proceeding collegiately; in this event, as has been noted above, they do not enjoy any right of precedence.[11]

The right to march in procession so that precedence may be enjoyed, is gained either through custom or invitation; hence a newly erected Tertiary Sodality must first prove its right to take part in a given procession before it can claim precedence in the same.[12]

Third Order Sodalities are not mentioned among those who are obliged to attend the yearly Corpus Christi procession from the principal church of the city: hence they are not obliged to attend this procession.[13]

Article II.

Indulgences of the Third Order Secular of St. Francis.

The Holy See has always been most generous in the large number of indulgences and other spiritual privileges she has always granted to the Third Order of St. Francis. It is not the purpose to enumerate them here, but rather to give the principal means of guidance in determining which indulgences accrue to Tertiaries and by what means they are available. Two of the more important ones will be given specifically.

§ 1. Sources of Indulgences.

By reason of their concession, indulgences and spiritual privileges are of a two-fold nature: those granted directly and those granted by communication. Therefore a distinc-

[11] Can. 703, § 3; 706.
[12] Gennari, *M. E.*, 4, Ser. III, vol. XXIV, 377, n. 34.
[13] Can. 1291, § 1.

tion must be drawn regarding those indulgences which are granted directly to the Third Order Secular of St. Francis, and those which are indirectly granted through the communication with the First Order and the Third Order Regular. The distinction must also be borne in mind between those granted to the Third Order as a whole, and those granted to Sodalities of the Third Order, for it is evident that a Tertiary who does not belong to a Sodality cannot take part in the special indulgences and privileges which are available to members of a Sodality, e. g. attendance at the monthly meetings of the Sodality.[1]

The communication of Pius X. Pius X, wishing to en-

[1] Cf. List of Indulgences attached to the *Rule of Leo XIII*, II, 2; above, p. 125-127. According to canon 692, one must be validly received into an association in order to partake in its indulgences and privileges. All authors treating on this legislation which existed both before and after the Code definitely assert that Tertiary novices belong to the Third Order in a manner which is sufficient for them to partake in its indulgences and privileges: and the more so, since the *Ceremonial of the Third Order* (Art. III) prescribes a definite mode of reception and registration. These commentators also logically deduce an analogy from canon 567, § 1, which gives this privilege to religious novices, and hence this can safely be asserted. However, just as *religious* novices cannot partake in those rights which are enjoyed only by *professed* members of a religious Institute (Vermeersch-Creusen, *Epitome*. n. 667), so also are the temporal rights of *Tertiary* novices restricted so that they have no right to partake in elections, receive offices in a Sodality, and in general concern themselves with the government of a Sodality, for Tertiary novices alone could not form a moral person known as a *Tertiary* Sodality, in the same manner as religious novices cannot form a *domus formata* (Can. 488, 5°): that they cannot concern themselves with the government and elections is also evident from the fact that the offices in a Sodality last for a period of three years (*Rule of Leo XIII*, III, § 1) while a Tertiary novice, as a novice, exists for only one year (*Ibidem*, I, § 1). Cf. Tischler, *Handbuch zur Leitung des Dritten Ordens*, p. 125; Holzapfel, *Die Leitung des Dritten Ordens*, p. 92; Tachy, *Les Tiers Ordres*, n. 64; Cerri, *Il Terz' Ordine Francescano*, p. 58; Mileta, *Trattato Giuridico sul Terz' Ordine Francescano*, p. 34.

rich the Third Order with many spiritual favors granted 'perpetually that all Franciscan Tertiaries, no matter of what sex or institute, participate both in life and in death in all favors granted through pontifical indulgence to the First and Second Order, as also in all the spiritual benefits derived from the good works of the latter.'[2]

Some doubt arose as to whether this communication was only between Tertiaries and those with whom they were affiliated, or between all Tertiaries and all religious of the First and Second Order. This doubt was cleared by a rescript of the same pontiff in which he states that the communication is reciprocal 'quatenus laudata Indulgentiarum et spiritualium fructuum mutua communicatione perfrui in perpetuum possint, quotquot sub Patriarche Seraphici S. Francisci vexillo militant ad quemcumque Ordinem vel Ordinis Familiam pertineant.'[3] From the tenor and words of the communication, it is clear that it is a communication *a jure*, and *in forma accessoria*.[4]

It is to be noted that this communication extends only to *indulgences* and not to *indults*, and therefore although through this communication Tertiaries have the right of receiving the blessing with plenary indulgence on the same days as it is imparted to the Franciscan Religious (the more proper term for that given to religious is General

[2] "* * * statuimus in perpetuum, ut quibus pontificalis indulgentiae donis fruuntur quosque de bonis operibus spirituales fructus percipiunt familiae seraphicae Primi et Alterius Ordinis, ea omnia Tertiarii Franciscales quotquot sunt utriusque sexus et cujusvi instituti, vitae mortisque tempore participent."—Brief, *Sodalium e Tertio Ordine*, May 5, 1909 (*A. M.*, XXVIII, 174-176).

[3] May 17, 1909 (*o. c.*, 177); both concessions were approved and declared authentic by the Congregation of the Holy Office, Dec. 20, 1910, and Jan. 18, 1911 (*o. c.*, XXX, 242 f).

[4] Cf. can. 65; *S. C. of the Holy office*, June 8, 1916, ad V (*A. A. S.*, VIII [1916], 264).

Absolution), nevertheless the Tertiaries cannot partake in the *indult* which the Franciscan religious enjoy of receiving this blessing on certain special days due to communication between the Families of the First Order; the reason for this is that Tertiaries participate in the *indulgences* of the other Franciscan Families, not in the *indults.*[5]

This communication is not only personal, but also local, so that churches and oratories belonging to secular Tertiaries enjoy the same indulgences as were granted to the First and Second, and the Third Order Regular in favor of the faithful who visit them on certain days.[6] A church or oratory where a Tertiary Sodality is situated, even though it does not properly belong to the Tertiaries, enjoys the same indulgences in favor of the Tertiaries visiting it, as those directly granted to Franciscan churches of the First and Second, and the Third Order Regular.[7]

The plenary indulgence granted to all Tertiaries who visit a church of the First Order on the feast of 'All Souls of the Order', can be gained only once yearly. The communication of Pius X is not to be understood that it can be gained by the Tertiaries on the different dates this feast is celebrated in the various Families of the First Order.[8]

Both by means of direct concession and through the communication of Pius X, the following are the principal sources of Indulgences which are available to Franciscan Tertiaries: The indulgences and privileges attached to the Rule of Leo XIII; (direct concession)[9] a Summary of Indulgences pertaining to the Seraphic Order, approved by

[5] Cf. Stein, *Tertius Ordo Franciscalis*, p. 76.

[6] *S. C. of the Holy Office*, June 8, 1916, ad I (*A. A. S.*, VIII [1916], 263 f).

[7] *Ibidem*, ad II.

[8] *Ibidem*, ad III.

[9] Given in the Const., *Misericors Dei Filius*, May 30, 1883 (*Fontes*, n. 588).

the S. C. of Indulgences July 20, 1841; (both direct concession and through communication),[10] the Summary approved by the same Congregation, Sept. 11, 1901; (direct concession),[11] the Summary of Indulgences and Privileges approved for the Friars Minor Capuchin, June 23, 1905 (direct concession and through communication);[12] the indulgencies contained in the Brief, *Qui multa*, of Leo XIII, Sept. 7, 1901.[13]

The small habit consisting of scapular and cord must be continually worn by the Tertiaries as a *conditio sine qua non* of gaining the indulgences and privileges of the Order; therefore during the time that they are not wearing these, they cannot partake in the indulgences and privileges: as soon as they reassume the scapular and cord, they automatically reassume these rights and privileges.[14] The Franciscan Superiors (and their delegated Director) may commute the wearing of the scapular into a medal so that Tertiaries wearing

[10] This may be found in Mocchegiani, *Collectio Indulgentiarum*, n. 1501; but the same Congregation, June 25, 1904, declared that this summary needed revision (Stein, *o. c.*, p. 77); hence care must be exercised in its use.

[11] This may be found in: *M. E.*, 3, Ser. II, vol. XIII, 391-397; Mocchegiani, *Jurisprudentia Ecclesiastica*, II, p. 443-449; Fleming, *Leonis XIII Acta ad III Ordinem Spectantia*, p. 229-235.

[12] *A. S. S.*, XXXVIII, 42-57; *M. E.*, 7, Ser. II, vol. XVII, 498-509; *Summarium Indulg. Privil. et Indult. Capucinorum*, Rome, 1905; *Analecta O. M. Cap.*, XXI, 228-235.

[13] *A. M.*, XX, 152-157.

[14] "Adlecti in sodalitatem scapulare parvum unaque cingulum de more gerant: ni gesserint, statis privilegiis juribusque careant." (*Rule of Leo XIII*, I §3); *S. S. of Indulgences*, May 27, 1857 (*Decreta Authentica S. C. Indulg.*, n 379); June 10, 1886 (*A. S. S.*, XIX, 44 f); this is a condition which the *Rule of the Third Order* mentions of those who belong to a *Sodality*: *a pari* the same is true of those who belong to the Third Order as a whole, for the scapular is not an insignia of a *Sodality* but of the Franciscan Third Order Secular *as a whole*.

such a medal partake of all the indulgences and privileges of the Order; this may be done only in individual cases, and a general commutation is forbidden.[15] The general observance of the Rules of an association is not a necessary requisite for participation in its indulgences and privileges, except in those things which are expressly mentioned.[16]

§ 2. Papal Blessing with Plenary Indulgence

According to the concession of Leo XIII, this blessing may be imparted to the Tertiaries twice a year;[17] it is not to be given on the same day or in the same place, i. e., in the same town or city in which the bishop imparts it.[18]

Under pain of invalidity, this blessing can be given only in the churches of the Regulars who have the authority to impart it, and in the Churches of the Tertiaries who are aggregated to these Regulars;[19] this latter is to be understood as the church or chapel where the Tertiary Sodality is canonically erected.[21]

[15] *S. C. of Religious,* March 25, 1922 (*A. A. S.*, XIV [1922], 353 f).

[16] Can. 692; cf. the declaration of the *S. C. of Indulgences,* Jan 25, 1842, ad II (*Decreta Authentica S. C. Indulg.*, n. 298).

[17] List of Indulgences attached to the Rule, I, § 3.

[18] Can. 915; Vermeersch-Creusen, *Epitome,* II, n. 209.

[19] *Ibidem.*

[21] a) This latter interpretation is entirely in harmony with canon 18 which states that in case of doubt the mind of the legislator should be sought: the majority of Tertiary Sodalities, if not erected in the Churches of the Friars Minor, are erected in secular or other regular parishes which do not belong to the Tertiaries; the mind of the legislator does not seem to be that these Tertiaries are to be deprived of the privilege of this blessing. b) The words of canon 915 'in ecclesiis Tertiarorum', do not forbid this interpretation as would the words 'in *propriis* ecclesiis Tertiariorum', for when the Holy See wishes the latter interpretation to be put on its words, it expressly states 'in *propriis* ecclesiis' or uses words similar to that effect which have not been used in the present instance: cf. *S. C. of the Holy Office,* May 28, 1914 (*Fontes,* n. 1297); the same Congregation, June 8, 1916, ad

Since the Superiors of the Friars Minor enjoy ordinary jurisdiction over the Tertiaries in spiritual matters, it is apparent that they can delegate the authority of giving the papal blessing to other priests: especially is this understood to be given to the Director. They can delegate any priest of the Order to give this blessing in their churches, even though this priest be not approved for confessions;[32] since no sacramental jurisdiction is required for imparting this blessing, it does not seem to be forbidden to delegate this faculty even to a priest outside of the Order who is not approved for confessions.

The papal blessing can be given only when the Tertiaries are congregated together;[33] the formula of Benedict XIV must be used under pain of invalidity.[34]

Directors of Tertiary Sodalities have the authority of giving this blessing without any further delegation on the part of the Franciscan Superiors;[35] they receive the benefit of the papal blessing at the same time as they impart it to the Tertiaries, provided they are legitimately impeded from receiving this blessing from another priest (with the required faculties) on the days prescribed, and that they ful-

I-II (*A. A. S.*, VIII [1916], 263 f). c) The Congregation of Indulgences has declared that the place for receiving this blessing is that place where the Sodality is canonically erected (Sept. 11, 1905, ad III (*M. E.*, 3, Ser. II, vol. XIII, 396), therefore since this privilege has not been expressly revoked by canon 915, it still retains its force (Can. 4).

[32] *S. C. of the Holy Office*, May 28, 1914 (*Fontes*, n. 1297; *A. A. S.*, VI [1914], 347).

[33] Benedict XIV, Const., *Exemplis praedecessorum*, March 19, 1748 §§ 9-10 (*Fontes*, n. 386); *Ceremonial of the Third Order*, Art. VIII.

[34] Leo XIII, Brief, *Quo Universi*, July 7, 1882 (*Fontes*, n. 586; *Decreta Authentica S. C. R.*, n. 2550); *S. C. of Indulgences, March 22*, 1879, ad VI (*Decreta Authentica S. C. Indulg.*, n. 444); this formula is given in the *Ceremonial of the Third Order*, l. c.

[35] *Ceremonial of the Third Order*, l. c.

fill the other necessary conditions.[26] In the event that Tertiaries are living in a place where no Sodality is canonically erected, they may receive the blessing with plenary indulgence in place of the papal blessing.[27] Tertiary priests who are impeded from attending at the papal blessing, may receive it on any day within the octave of the feast for which it is prescribed.[28] Tertiaries can receive this blessing either from their proper Director, or from a Director of a Sodality which is under the jurisdiction of a Franciscan obedience different from their own Sodality.[29]

The conditions for acquiring the plenary indulgence attached to this blessing are the following: confession, communion, and prayers according to the intention of the Roman pontiff.[30]

§ 3. The Blessing with Plenary Indulgence

In addition to the days on which this blessing may be imparted to the Tertiaries by direct concession, through the communication of Pius X, Tertiaries have the privilege of receiving this blessing on the same days on which general absolution is granted to the Franciscan Religious Families. The blessing which is applied to the latter however has the added effect of absolving from censure, while that given to the Secular Tertiaries is simply a blessing with plenary indulgence. Hence the former is correctly termed general

[26] *S. C. of Indulgences*, July 14, 1900 (*M. E.*, 2, Ser. II, vol. XII, 349 f).

[27] *S. C. of Indulgences*, Sept. 11, 1901, ad III (*o. c.*, 3, Ser. II, vol. XIII, 396.

[28] *S. C. of Indulgences*, Feb. 11, 1903 (*A. S. S.*, XXXV, 636 f); this seems to be the only instance where this blessing is allowed to be given outside of the prescribed time and without the Tertiaries being congregated together.

[29] *S. C. of Indulgences*, Jan. 30, 1896, ad III (*M. E.*, 9, Ser. I, vol. IX, 153).

[30] List of Indulgences attached to the *Rule of Leo XIII*, I, § 8.

absolution, and the latter, a blessing with plenary indulgence, although both terms are promiscuously used in referring to the privilege of the Tertiaries;[47] but from the words of the formula it is evident that this promiscuous use of the term is inaccurate.[48]

This blessing is to be given by the Franciscan Superiors or by those delegated by them; the Director of a Sodality has this authority *ex officio* without any delegation.[49] The Franciscan Superiors can delegate any priest of their Order to give this blessing in their churches, even though he be not approved for confessions.[50] There seems to be no reason why it could not also be given to a priest outside of the Order who is not approved for confessions. In the event that the Tertiaries are congregated for the blessing and the priest with the required faculties does not appear, any priest whether regular or secular who is approved for hearing confessions, may impart the blessing.[51]

Ordinarily the blessing is to be given publicly, i. e., the Tertiaries being congregated together,[52] by a priest vested in violet stole[53] using the formula beginning with the words 'Intret oratio mea' under pain of invalidity.[54]

[47] Cf. *S. C. of the Holy Office,* Dec. 15, 1910 (*Fontes,* n. 1289); May 28, 1914 (*o. c.,* n. 1297); List of Indulgences attached to the Rule of Leo XIII, I, § 8; *S. C. of Indulgences,* March 22, 1842, ad I (*Decreta Authentica S. C. Indulg.,* n. 444).

[48] Cf. *Ceremonial of the Third Order,* Art. IX.

[49] *S. C. of Indulgences,* July 14, 1900 (*M. E.,* 2, Ser. II, vol. XII, 350).

[50] *S. C. of the Holy Office,* May 28, 1914 (*Fontes,* n. 1297).

[51] *S. C. of the Holy Office,* Dec. 15, 1910 (*o. c.,* 1289).

[52] *S. C. of Rites,* Dec. 22, 1905 (*Decreta Authentica S. C. R.,* n. 4176); *S. C. of Indulgences,* July 21, 1888 (*M. E.,* 5, Ser. I, vol V, 153).

[53] *S. C. of Rites,* Dec. 22, 1905, l. c.

[54] Leo XIII, Brief, *Quo Universi,* July 7, 1882 (*Fontes,* n. 586); *S. C. of Rites,* June 17, 1919, ad II (*A. M.,* XXXVIII, 230).

When Tertiaries are present at the time the general absolution is given to the Franciscan Religious in a church or oratory under the formula *'Ne reminiscaris',*[55] they receive the benefit of the plenary indulgence and also the absolution from censure. In the same manner, Franciscan Religious who are grouped together with the Secular Tertiaries at the time that the blessing with plenary indulgence is imparted to the Tertiaries under the formula *'Intret oratio mea',* also gain the effect of a plenary indulgence with absolution from censure.[56]

The blessing may be received from a Director who is of a different obedience than that to which one's Sodality is subject;[57] directors who are legitimately impeded from receiving this blessing from another priest on the days prescribed, receive the benefit of the blessing in the act of imparting it to the Tertiaries, provided they fulfill the other conditions;[58] the blessing may be given publicly or privately on any day of the octave of the feast for which it is assigned,[59] privately also on the day before the feast.[60] This

[55] Prescribed by Leo XIII, l. c.

[56] *S. C. of Rites,* June 7, 1919 (*A. M.*, l. c.).

[57] *S. C. of Indulgences,* Jan. 30, 1896, ad III (*M. E.*, 9, Ser. I, vol. IX, 153).

[58] *S. C. of Indulgences,* July 14, 1900 (*M. E.*, 2, Ser. II, vol. XII, 349).

[59] Benedict XV, Apr. 14, 1917 (*A. A. S.*, IX [1917], 262); this decree does not abrogate the one immediately preceding or render it useless; the concession of being able to receive the blessing either publicly or privately within the octave of the feast for which it is assigned is a privilege in favor of the *invidual* and therefore does not need to be employed (can. 69). Hence since the later decree does not revoke the former, a priest who is legitimately impeded from receiving this blessing from another on the day prescribed for the blessing, may refuse to avail himself of the privilege of the octave and receive the effect of the blessing in the act of imparting it to the Tertiaries. Besides it may

blessing in private may be given by any priest approved for confessions, but must be imparted in a place approved for the hearing of confessions,[61] although it is not necessary that the blessing be immediately connected with the sacrament.[62]

The place for imparting this blessing privately is to be understood according to canons 908-910: the proper place for hearing confessions is in a church, or at least a semi-public oratory; confessions of men may also be heard in private homes; the confessional for women should always be in an open and conspicuous place, and generally in a church, or at least a public or semi-public oratory, with a firmly fixed perforated screen between the penitent and the confessor; the confessions of women should not be heard outside of these places except in case of infirmity or some other necessity, always observing the safeguards which the ordinary of the place may prescribe. Since the blessing with plenary indulgence is to be given privately in the place for hearing confessions, these prescriptions of the Code should be applied in the same manner.

The formula for imparting this blessing both publicly and privately is contained in the *Ceremonial of the Third Order,* Art. IX and in the appendix ad *Rituale Romanum,* 135*f.

happen in rural districts that a Director may not find the opportunity of receiving this blessing from another priest even within the octave.

[60] *S. C. of Indulgences,* July 21, 1888 (*M. E.,* 5, Ser. I, vol. V, 153); *S. C. of the Holy Office,* June 12, 1913 (*A. A. S.,* V [1913], 306 f)

[61] *S. C. of Indulgences,* July 21, 1888, l. c.; Jan. 30, 1896, ad I-II (*M. E.,* 9, Ser. I, vol. IX, 152 f).

[62] The decree of 1888 states that it is to be given 'post expletam confessionem'; however confession is necessary for the valid reception of the indulgence (List of Indulgences attached to the Rule of Leo XIII, I), and therefore the Congregation is only repeating one of the conditions already stipulated, i. e. that confession is necessary. The decree of 1906 omits any mention of confession, and only repeats that it must of necessity be given in a place approved for confessions.

The list of Indulgences attached to the Rule of Leo XIII demands the same conditions for gaining this indulgence as for the papal blessing: confession, communion and prayers for the intention of the pontiff.

Article III

Indults granted to the Third Order Secular of St. Francis

A number of indults have already been mentioned in their special relation to the papal blessing and the blessing with plenary indulgence. Canonically speaking, indults do not come under the caption of indulgences, but since they are intimately connected with these blessings, and their application is necessary for the understanding of the same, they have been mentioned in immediate connection with those indulgences for the extension and the interpretation of which the Holy See has given them. Hence the reason for placing them under the heading of indulgences, rather than indults.

The following are the more important indults granted to the Third Order Secular of St. Francis:

a) Tertiary priests enjoy the indult of a personal privileged altar three days of each week, no matter where they celebrate Mass, provided they do not ask a similar indult for another day.[1]

b) All Masses which are celebrated for the repose of the souls of deceased Tertiaries are privileged.[2]

c) Tertiary priests, even though canonically bound to the service of some church, may use the Romano-Seraphic Calendar in the recitation of the Divine Office, provided they are

[1] List of Indulgences attached to the Rule of Leo XIII, III, § 1.

[2] Summarium indulgentiarum, privilegiorum ac indultorum, approved by the S. C. of Indulgences, Sept. 11, 1901 (VI, 1).

not bound to choir;[3] they should use the Calendar of the obedience to which they are subject as Tertiaries; they also partake of the privilege granted to the three First Orders of reading a votive Mass of the Immaculate Conception on every Saturday of the year which is not impeded by: a double of the first or second class, a vigil, the time of Quadregesima, Ember days, or a feast of the Blessed Virgin; this Mass must be celebrated in a church pertaining to one of the three First Orders, or in a private oratory.[4]

d) Tertiaries who are infirm or convalescing and cannot conveniently (commode) leave their homes, may recite five Our Fathers and Hail Marys together with prayers for the intention of the sovereign pontiff and thus gain the same indulgences as those attached to a visit to a church of the Franciscan Religious Orders or a Sodality.[5] This indult is applicable to the indulgences which have been given by direct concession to visits to these churches, as well as those comprehended in the communication of Pius X.[6]

e) Tertiaries may gain all the indulgences granted to the faithful for visiting Franciscan Churches as well as those which are proper to the Third Order Secular, under the condition that they visit the parish church in those places where there is neither a Franciscan church or a public oratory of the Third Order Secular, or a church where a Sodality is canonically erected.[7]

[3] *S. C. of Rites,* Apr. 14, 1904 (*Decreta Authentica S. C. R.,* n. 4132).

[4] *S. C. of Rites,* March 22, 1905 (*A. S. S.,* XXXVIII, 40 f).

[5] Summarium indulgentiarum, privilegiorum ac Indultorum, approved by the S. C. of Indulgences, Sept. 11, 1901 (V, 5); can. 935 gives authority to the confessor to commute the pious works prescribed for gaining an indulgence, provided the conditions cannot be observed.

[6] *S. C. of the Holy Office,* June 8, 1916, ad IV (*A. A. S.,* VIII [1916], 264).

[7] Summarium indulgentiarum, privilegiorum ac indultorum, approved by the S. C. of Indulgences, Sept. 11, 1901 (V, 6).

f) Those indulgences which are gained for visiting Franciscan churches of the First and Second Order and the Third Order Regular, may be gained by the Tertiaries by visiting a church or a chapel where a Sodality is canonically erected.[8]

g) Secular Tertiaries living in seminaries, hospitals, colleges, prisons and other similar places which have a semipublic oratory, by visiting the same, can gain the same indulgences as are attached to visiting: the parish, a church of the First Order, that in which a Sodality is erected, or a public oratory of the Third Order, provided they are morally impeded from visiting the latter places.[9]

h) Tertiaries who gather for the monthly conference—the Director being absent on account of sacerdotal duties—recite the accustomed prayers, and hear a sermon in place of the conference, may gain the indulgence attached to attendance at the monthly conference, provided they are congregated with the authority of the Director.[10]

[8] *S. C. of the Holy Office*, June 6, 1916 (*A. A. S.*, VIII [1916], 264).
[9] *S. C. of Indulgences*, July 18, 1902, ad I (*A. S. S.*, XXXV, 63).
[10] *S. C. of Indulgences*, Jan. 30, 1896, ad VI (*M. E.*, 9, Ser. I, vol. IX, 153).

Appendix

Rules of the Third Order

The original Rule of 1221 which follows is that which is referred to repeatedly in this dissertation. It is given here in extenso as a ready reference for the various assertions concerning the development of the Order itself and its Rule. The Rule of Nicholas IV in 1289 is omitted because it is easily accessible and few references have been made to it throughout this work. That of Leo XIII in 1883 is also given here on account of the great number of times it has been cited.

Incipit Regula et vita Fratrum vel Sororum Paenitentium[1]

I. De modo vestium

1. Viri qui hujus fraternitatis fuerint de panno humili sine colore induantur cujus brachium sex soldorum Raven. pretium non excedat, nisi propter causam evidentem et necessariam, ad tempus, cum aliquo dispensetur. Et consideretur panni latitudo et arctitudo circa praedictum pretium. 2. Chlamydes et pelles habeant sine Scollatura fixas vel integras non tamen affiblatas ut portant saeculares et manicas clausas. 3. Sorores vero de ejusdem pretii panno et humilitatis chlamydes induantur et tunicas vel saltem cum chlamyde habeant guarnellum sive placentinum album vel nigrum aut amplum palutellum lineum sine crispaturis cujus brachium non exedat XII. den. Raven.; 4. de quo tamen pretio et de pellitionibus ipsarum dispensare poterit secumdum conditionem cujuscumque mulieris et loci consuetudi-

[1] Sabatier, *Regula antiqua Fratrum et Sororum de Paenitentia* (*Opuscules de Critique Historique*, I, 17-30); the italics are from the original author.

nem. 5. Bindas vel ligaturas sericas sive coloratas non portent, et tam fratres quam sorores pelles habeant agninas tantum. 6. Bursas de corio et corrigias sine serico consutas et non alias habere liceat. Et alia ornamenta visitatoris arbitrio deponant. 7. Ad convivia inhonesta, vel spectacula, vel choreas non vadant, histrionibus non donent et donari a familia prohibeant.

II. De abstinentia

1. Omnes abstineant a carnibus excepta dominica et tertia et quinta feria, nisi propter infirmitatem, debilitatem, minutionem tribus diebus et in itinere, 2. vel propter praecipuam solemnitatem intervenientem, scilicet nativitatis Domini per tres dies, anni novi, Epiphaniae, Paschae Resurrectionis per tres dies, apostolorum Petri et Pauli, nativitatis beati Johannis Baptistae, Assumptionis gloriosae Virginis Mariae, festi Omnium Sanstorum et sancti Martini. 3. Aliis vero diebus non jejunandis liceat comedere caseum et ova. Sed cum religiosis in eorum conventibus de appositis ab eis comedere licebit. 4. Et sint contenti prandio et cena, exceptis languidis et infirmis, viatoribus. Sanis cibus et potus sit temperatus. 5. Ante prandium et cenam dicant semel *Pater Noster,* post comestionem semel et gratias agant Domino. Alioquin dicant ter *Pater Noster.* 6. A Paschate Resurrectionis usque ad festum Omnium Sanctorum jejunent sexta feria. A festo Omnium Sanstorum usque ad Pascha quarta et Sexta feria jejunabunt, servantes nihilominus alia jejunia quae ab ecclesia indicantur generaliter facienda.

III. De jejuniis

1. Quadragesima vero sancti Martini post eamdem diem usque ad Natale et quadragesimam majorem a dominica carnisprivii usque ad Pascha continue jejunent, nisi propter infirmitateem vel aliam necessitatem. 2. Sorores gravidae

usque ad suam purificationem ab exercitationibus corporalibus exceptis vestibus et orationibus poterunt abstinere. 3. Laborantibus in fatigationibus a Paschate Resurrectionis usque ad sancti Michaelis dedicationem in die ter liceat cibum sumere. 4. Et quando alliis laborant de omnibus appositis comedere licebit excepta sexta feria et jejuniis ab ecclesia generaliter indictis.

IV. De orationibus

1. Omnes dicant quotidie septem horas canonicas vadelicet matutinum, primam, tertiam, sextam, nonam, vesperum et completorium; 2. clerici, sedundum ordinem clericorum; scientes psalterium, pro prima *Deus in nomine tuo* et *Beati immaculati* usque ad *Legen pone* et alios psalmos horarum cum *Gloria Patri* dicant. 3. Sed quum ad ecclesiam non vadunt, dicant pro matutino psalmos quos dicit Ecclesia vel alios quoscumque XVIII psalmos vel saltem *Pater Noster,* ut illiterati. 4. In omnibus horis aliis pro matutino XII *Pater Noster* et pro unaquaque alia hora septem *Pater Noster* cum *Gloria Patri* post unumquodque. 5. Et qui sciunt *Credo in Deum* et *Miserere mei Deus* in prima et completorio dicant, si non dixerint horis constitutis, dicant tamen *Pater Noster.* Infirmi non dicant horas nisi velint.

V. Quando ire debent ad matutinum

1. Omnes ad matutinum vadant in quadragesima sancti Martini et majori nisi personarum vel rerum incommoditas immineret.

VI. De confessione et communione et aliorum satisfactione et de armis non sumendis et juramentis non praestandis

1. Confessionem de peccatis faciant ter in anno et communionem in nativitate Domini et Paschate Resurrectionis et Pentecosten recipiant.

2. De decimis praeteritis satisfaciant et de futuris praestent.

3. Arma mortalia contra quempiam non recipiant vel secum ferant.

4. Omnes a juramentis solemnibus abstineant nisi necessitate cogente in casibus a summo pontifice exceptis in sua indulgentia vadelicet pro pace, fide, calumnia et testimonio.

5. Et in eorum loquela sicut poterunt vitabunt juramenta. Et qui incaute juraverit lapsu linguae, ut in multiloquo contingit, eadem in sero, quum recogitare debeant quod fecerint, pro talibus juramentis dicant ter *Pater Noster*.

6. Quisque suam familiam confortet ad serviendum Deo.

VII. De missa et congregatione cujusque mensis

1. Omnes fratres et sorores cujuscumque civitatis et loci quolibet mense quandocumque videbitur expedire conveniant apud ecclesiam quam ministri nuntiaverint, ibique audiant divina. 2. Et quilibet det massario unum denarium usualem quos idem massarius colligat et ministrorum consilio inter fratres pauperes et sorores distribuat, et maxime infirmis et eis qui non habuerint funeris exsequias. Demum inter alios pauperes et eidem ecclesiae de eadem pecunia offerat. 3. Et tunc, si commode possunt, habeant unum religiosum in Dei verbo instructum qui eos moneat et confortet ad paenitentiam, perseverantiam et opera misericordiae facienda. 4. Et sint sub silentia in missa et praedicatione, intenti officio, orationi et praedicationi, exceptis officialibus.

VIII. De operibus misericordiae et testimentis et discordiis reformandis

1. Quum aliquem fratrum vel sororum contigerit infirmari ministri per se vel per alios si infirmus eis fecerit nuntiari semel in hebdomada visitent infirmantem et ad paenitentiam

commoveant et sicut viderint expedire necessaria corporis quibus indiget de communi administrent.

IX. De fratribus defunctis

1. Et si de hac luce migraverit infirmatus nuntietur fratribus et sororibus qui fuerint in civitate vel loco praesentes ut ad ipsius conveniant sepulturam nec recedant donec missa fuerit celebrata et corpus traditum sepulturae. 2. Et post, quilibet, infra octo dies defunctionis ipsius, dicat pro anima defuncti, presbyter missam, sciens psalterium quinquaginta psalmos, alii quinquaginta *Pater Noster* cum *Requiem aeternam* in fine cujusque. 3. Praeter haec infra annum pro salute fratrum et sororum vivorum et mortuorum dicat presbyter tres missas, sciens psalterium dicat ipsum, alii dicant centum *Pater Noster* cum *Requiem aeternam* in fine cujuslibet. Alioquin duplicent.

X. De testamentis faciendis

1. Omnes qui possunt de jure testamentum faciant et de rebus suis infra tres menses post promissionem disponant, ne quis ipsorum intestatus decedat.

2. De pace inter fratres et sorores aut extraneos discordes facienda, sicut ministris videbitur, sic fiat; habito etiam si expedierit consilio episcopi dioecesani.

3. Si contra jus vel privilegia fratres vel sorores a potestatibus vel rectoribus locorum in quibus habitant vexentur, ministri loci quod videbitur expedire cum consilio domini episcopi faciant.

4. Ministerium et alia officia quae sunt hic scripta sibi imposita quilibet suscipiat et fideliter exerceat, dum tamen per annum ab officio vacare quilibet possit.

5. Quum aliquis huic fraternitati intrare petierit, ministri ejus conditionem et officium inquirant et onera fraternitatis hujus et maxime alienorum restitutionem exponant ei.

6. Et si placuerit ei secundum praedictum modum, induatur, et de alienis satisfaciat, numerata pecunia vel cautione pignoris data. Proximis se reconciliet et de decimis satisfaciat. 7. Quibus impletis post annum cum consilio aliquorum discretorum fratrum, si eis idoneus videbitur, recipiatur hoc modo: 8. Quod promittat se observare omnia quae hic sunt scripta, sive scribenda, vel minuenda, secundum consilium fratrum toto tempore vitae suae, nisi aliquando de licentia stetit ministrorum. 9. Et quod si quid contra hunc modum fecerit, interpellatus a ministris, satisfaciat ad voluntatem visitatoris. 10. Et per manum publicam promissio in scriptis redigatur ibidem. 11. Nemo tamen aliter recipiatur, nisi aliter eis visum fuerit considerata personae conditione et ejus instantia.

12. De hac fraternitate et de iis quae hic continentur nemo exire valeat nisi religionem ingrediatur.

XI. De contemptione et suspicatione haereticorum

1. Nullus haereticus vel de haeresi diffamatus recipiatur. Si autem suspectus sollumodo fuerit, purgatus coram episcopo, si alias idoneus fuerit, admittatur.
consensu et licentia maritorum.

2. Mulieres vero viros habentes non recipientur nisi de

3. Incorrigibiles fratres et sorores a fraternitate ejecti iterum in ea nullo modo recipiantur, nisi saniori parti fratum placuerit.

XII. De culpis dicendis

1. Ministri cujuslibet civitatis et loci culpas fratrum et sororum manifestas nuntient visitatori puniendas. 2. Et si aliquis incorrigibilis extiterit, per ministros, habito consilio alquorum discretorum fratrum eidem visitatori intimetur ab ipso de fraternitate abjiciendus et in congregatione publice-

tur. 3. Insuper, si est frater, potestati loci vel rectori denuntietur.

4. Si quis sciverit de fratribus vel sororibus aliquem scandalum facere ministris nuntiet et visitatori valeat nuntiare et quod inter virum et uxorem non teneantur.

5. Visitator cum fratribus universis in iis omnibus potestatem habeant dispensandi quum viderint expedire.

6. Ministri cum consilio suorum fratrum post annum eligant duos alios ministros et fidelem massarium qui necessitati fratrum et sororum et aliorum pauperum provideat et nuntios qui dicta factaque fraternitatis de mandata eorum nuntiet.

7. In supradictis omnibus nemo obligetur ad culpam sed ad poenam, ita tamen quod si poenam a visitatore impositam vel imponendam, bis admonitus a ministris, exsolvere neglexerit, tamquam contumax obligatur ad culpam.

XIII. De culpis manifestandis

1. Statuimus quod nullus faciat fidejussionem pro aliquo, nisi forte pro aliquo de ista fraternitate, et hoc etiam fiat de licentia visitatoris vel ministrorum.

2. Item visitator de consensu ministrorum et aliorum fratrum dat licentiam fratribus non eundi ad ecclesiam aliquo tempore, dummodo bene dicat matutinum et alias horas suas.

3. Item quilibet frater confiteatur alicui sacerdoti semel in quolibet mense, quia in sancta confessione omnia lavantur et major gratia Dei datur.

4. Item visitator et ministri hujus fraternitatis petant a ministro vel custode fratrum Minorum unum fratrem Minorem de conventu, cujus fratris consilio et voluntate fratrum ista fraternitas gubernetur in omnibus et regatur. 5. Et quando ille frater recederet de conventu, petant alium loco ejus, ita quod semper consilio fratrum Minorum regatur ista fraternitas quae a beato Francisco habuit fundamentum.

6. Item omnes fratres conveniant in prima dominica cujuslibet mensis ad missam in loco fratrum Minorum, nisi remaneant, de licentia visitatoris vel ministrorum, propter aliquam legitimam causam. Et similiter eodem die conveniant ibidem post nonam. 7. Item si visitator vel ministri non poterunt interesse in die quando ista fraternitas congregatur, aliqua causa legitima impediente, quilibet eorum faciat unum vicarium loco sui qui tunc ejus officium exerceat, ita quod sancta fraternitas non contingat propter hoc inpediri.

8. Item quicumque fratrum istius fraternitatis fecerit publice aliquid scandalum vel aliquem excessum accuset seipsum de hoc publice coram omnibus fratribus in die quando fratres conveniunt. 9. Et si non se accusaverit, alius frater qui scit excessum, illum accuset in publico, et per visitatorem vel ministros vel eorum vicarios illi qui fecit excessum paenitentia cum misericordia imponatur, nisi sit talis excessus propter quem sit ille qui peccaverit de ordine expellendus.

10. Item nulla nova constitutio fiat nisi de majoris partis hujus fraternitatis consilio et assensu.

11. Item si quis ordinem nostrum intrare voluerit si tenetur restituere alicui personae aliquid male acquisitum restituat ei vel ejus haeredibus si cognoscit eos. 12. Si autem dubitat utrum habeat de illicite acquisitis sed nescit cui et quantum restituere teneatur faciat praeconizari per terram, ut moris est, vel in praedicatione solemni diei, quod ipse paratus est satisfacere omnibus quibuscumque quocumque modo aliquid satisfacere teneatur.

13. Item nullus frater deponat querimoniam coram potestate vel alio judice pro re aliqua vel injuria contra fratrem aliquem vel sororem de ordine nostro, nisi forte de licentia visitatoris et ministrorum suorum et majoris et sanioris partis loci consilio et assensu. 14. Sed volumus et statuimus quod si aliqua causa vel controversia seu discordia fuerit inter fratres quacumque de causa per visitatorem et minis-

tros, habito si oportuerit aliquorum discretorum consilio, terminetur. 15. Et quidquid visitator et ministri diffinierint, ut est dictum, fratres illi inter quos causa versabitur teneantur firmiter observare, ita quod inter religiosos et saeculares de fratribus nostris, auctore Deo, nullum scandalum oriatur. Explicit.

Rule of the Third Order Secular of St. Francis approved by Leo XIII, May 30, 1883.[1]

LEX

SODALIUM FRANCISCALIUM TERTII ORDINIS QUI *SAECULARIS* DICITUR

CAP. I

De cooptatione, tirocinio, professione

§1. Ne quos cooptari liceat, nisi majores quatuordecim annorum, eosque bene moratos, retinentes concordiae, atque in primis sanctitate professionis catholicae probatos, spectatoque erga Ecclesiam Romanam Sedemque Apostolicam obsequio.

§2. Nuptae, nisi sciente et consentiente viro, ne cooptentur, extra quam si secus videatur faciendum, auctore sacerdote conscientiae ipsarum judice.

§3. Adlecti in sodalitatem *scapulare* parvum unaque cingulum de more gerant: ni gesserint, statis privilegiis juribusque careant.

[1] This was issued in the Constitution, *Misericors Dei Filius*, and is contained in the *Fontes*, n. 588; A. S. S., XV, 513-520; *Leonis XIII Acta*, III, 230-238; Fleming, *Leonis XIII Acta ad III Ordinem spectantia*, 72-87; only the Rule itself will be given here: the Constitution of approval as well as the list of Indulgences attached to the Rule will be omitted. Italics are as given in the *Fontes*.

§4. Qui quaeve Tertium Ordinem inierint, unum ipsum annum tirocinio exigant: mox, Ordinem rite professi, servaturos sese jura Dei, obedientes Ecclesiae dicto futuros; si quid in iis, quae professi sunt, deliquerint, satis facturos singuli spondeant.

CAP. II.

De Disciplina Vivendi

§1. Sodales Tertii Ordinis in omni cultu habituque, sumptuosiore elegantia posthabita, teneant eam, quae singulos deceat, mediocritatis regulam.

§2. Choreis ludisve scenicis procacioribus, item commissationibus perquam caute abstineant.

§3. Pastu atque potu utantur frugaliter: neve ante vel accumbant vel assurgant de mensa, quam invocato pie grateque Deo.

§4. Jejunium Mariae Virgini Immaculatae, item Francisco Patri, pridie sacra solemnia, singuli servanto: admodum laudabiles, si qui praeterea vel jejunium in sextas, vel abstinentiam carnium in quartas quasque ferias servarint, disciplina veteri Tertiariorum.

§5. Admissa rite expianto per menses singulos: item ad divinum epulum accedant per menses singulos.

§6. Tertiarios ex ordine Clericorum, quod Psalmis quotidie dant operam, nihil praeterea hoc nomine debere placet. Laici, qui nec canonicas, neu Mariales preces, vulgo *Officium parvum B. M. V.*, persolvunt, precationem Dominicam cum Salutatione Angelica et *Gloria Patri* adhibeant duodecies in dies singulos, excepto si per valetudinem non liceat.

§7. Quibus est testamenti factio, ii suo quisque tempore de re sua testentur.

§8. In familiari vita studeant ceteros exemplo antecedere: pietatis artes, resque optimas provehere. Libros vel diaria, unde pernicies virtuti metuatur, domum suam inferri, ab iisque, qui in ipsorum potestate sint, legi ne sinant.

§9. Caritatem benevolam et inter se et ad alienos sedulo tueantur. Componendas, sicubi possunt, discordias curent.

§10. Jusjurandum ne jurant umquam, nisi necessario. Turpia dictu, scurriles jocos fando fugiant. Excutiant sese vesperi, num tale quidquam temere fecerint: si fecerint, errorem poentitendo corrigiant.

§11. Rei divinae, qui commode possunt, quotidie intersint. Ad coetus menstruos, quos Praefectus indixerit, conveniant.

§12. Conferant in commune pro facultate quisque sua nonnihil, unde vel tenuiores e sodalium numero, presertim affecta valetudine, subleventur, vel divini cultus dignitati consulatur.

§13. Ad sodalem aegrotantem Praefecti vel adeant ipsi, vel mittant, qui caritatis officia expleat. Iidem, in morbo ancipiti, moneant suadeant, ut quae ad expiandum animum pertinent, aegrotus tempestive curet.

§14. Ad exsequias sodalis demortui sodales municipes hospitesve conveniant, simulque Mariales preces instituto Dominici Patris, id est *Rosarium,* tertiam partem ad caeleste demortui solatium adhibeant. Item sacerdotes inter rem divinam, laici, si poterunt, sumpta Eucharistia, pacem fratri defuncto sempiternam pii volentes adprecentur.

CAP. III.

De Officiis, De Visitatione, deque Ipsa Lege

§1. Officia, advocatis ad conventum sodalibus, deferantur. Eadem trinealia sunto. Oblata ne qui sine caussa justa recuset, neu oscitanter gerat.

§2. Curator, qui *Visitator* audit, diligenter quaerat, satisne salvae leges. Eius rei ergo, sodalitiorum sedes in singulos annos, eoque crebrius, si res postulaverit, pro potestate circumeat, coetumque habeat, Praefectis sodalibusque universis adesse jussis. Si quem *Visitator* ad officium monendo jubendo revocarit, sive quid, salutaris poenae nomine, in quemquam decreverit, hic modeste accipiat, idemque luere ne abnuat.

§3. *Visitatores* ex Primo Franciscalium Ordine, vel ex Ordine Tertio Regulari legantur, quos Custodes seu *Guardiani,* si id rogati fuerint, designabunt. *Visitatoris* munere laicis viris interdictum esto.

§4. Sodales nec obedientes et noxii iterum et tertium admoneantur officii sui: ni pareant, excedere Ordine jubeantur.

§5. In his legibus si qui forte quid deliquerint, hoc se nomine culpam suscepturos nullam sciant, exceptis iis quae jure divino Ecclesiaeque legibus alioqui praecipiuntur.

§6. Si quae hujus capita legis quemquam servare caussa gravis et justa prohibeat, eum ex ea parte lege solvi, eademve capita commutari prudenter liceat. Cujus rei Praefectis ordinariis Franciscalium et Primi Ordinis et Tertii item *Visitatoribus* supra dictis facultas potestasque sit.

BIBLIOGRAPHY

I. Sources

A. A. S.-Acta Apostolicae Sedis, Romae, 1909-.

A. S. S.-Acta Sanctae Sedis, 41 vols., Romae, 1865-1908.

A. M.-Acta Ordinis Minorum vel ad Ordinem quoque modo pertinentia, Quaracchi, 1882.

Analecta Juris Pontificii, Série 1-28, Paris, 1855-1888.

Analecta Ordinis Minorum Capucinorum, Romae, 1884-.

Bull. Franc.-Bullarium Franciscanum Romanorum Pontificum, ed. Sbaralea, O. M. Conv., vol. I-III, Romae, 1761-1768; vol. IV-VII, ed. Eubel, O. M. Conv., Romae 1898-1902 et Quaracchi, 1904.

Bullarii Frasciscani Epitome et Supplementum, ed. Eubel, O. M. Conv., Quaracchi, 1908.

Bullarium Ordinis Fratrum Minorum S. Francisci Capuccinorum seu Collectio Bullarum, Brevium, Decretorum, Rescriptorum, et Oraculorum . . . qua a S. Sede Apostolica pro Ordine Capuccino emanarunt, vol. I-IX, Romae, 1740-1884.

Bullarium Ordinis Praedicatorum sub auspiciis SS. D. N. D. Benedicti XIII . . . editum, vol. I, Romae, 1729.

Bull. Rom.-Bullarium, Diplomatum et Privilegiorum Sanctorum Romanorum Pontificum, Taurinensis editio, . . . auspicante Cardinale Francisco Gaude, 24 vols., Augustae Taurinorum, 1857-1882.

Bullarii Romani Continuatio Summorum Pontificum, 19 vols., Prati, 1756-1892.

Butler, *Regula Monastica*, Freiburg, 1912.

Caeremoniale Tertii Ordinis S. P. Francisci a Sacra Rituum Congregatione Approbatum (die 8 Junii, 1883) (Fleming, *Leonis XIII Acta ad III Oidinem Spectantia*, p. 197-222).

Canones et Decreta Sacrosancti et Oecumenici Concilii Tridentini, Taurini, 1913.

Codex Juris Canonici PII X Pontificis Maximi jussu digestus Benedicti Papae XV auctoritate promulgatus, Romae, 1917.

Collectanea S. Congregationis de Propaganda Fide, seu Decreta, Instructiones, Rescripta pro apostolicis missionibus, 2 vols., Romae, 1907.

Commentarium Ordinis Fratum Minorum S. Francisci Conventualium, Romae, 1903-.

Constitutiones Urbanae Ordinis Minorum Conventualium S. P. Francisci, Mechlinae, 1880.

Corpus Juris Canonici, Editio Lipsiensis II (Richter-Friedberg), 2 vols., Leipsic, 1922.

Decreta Authentica Congregationis Sacrorum Rituum, 7 vols., Romae, 1898-1927.

Decreta Authentica Sacrae Congregationis Indulgentiis Sacrisque Reliquiis praepositae ab anno 1668 ad annum 1882 edita jussu et auctoritate Leonis XIII, Ratisbonae, Neo Eboraci & Cincinnatii, 1883.

Denziger, Henricus, et Bannwart, Clemens, *Enchiridion Symbolorum,* quam paravit, J. B. Umberg, S. J., 14 and 15 ed., Friburgi Brisgoviae, 1922.

Fontes Codicis Juris Canonici, 4 vols., Romae, 1923-1926.

Leonis XIII Acta, 23 vols., Romae, 1881-1905.

Leonis XIII Acta ad III Franciscalem Ordinem Spectantia collecta . . . auctoritate Rmi P. D. Fleming, O. F. M., Quaracchi, 1901.

Mansi, J. D., *Sacrorum Conciliorum nova et amplissima collectio,* 50 vols., Parisiis, 1902.

Migne, P. J., *Patrologia Latina,* Parisiis, 1858-1864.

M.E.-Monitore Ecclesiastico, II, Maratea, 1876-.

Orbis Seraphicus ed. Dom. de Gubernatis, O. F. M., vol. II, Romae, 1685.

Proprium Officiorum ad usum Fratrum Minorum Conventualium . . ., Romae, 1924.

Regola del Terz' Ordine Claustrale di S. Francesco D'Assisi, Roma, 1889.

Regula et Constitutiones Fratrum Minorum Capuccinorum, Romae, 1926.

Regula et Constitutiones Generales Fratrum Minorum, Quaracchi, 1922.

Rescripta Authentica Sacrae Congregationis Indulgentiis Sacrisque Reliquiis praepositae . . . quae . . . contulit Josephus Schneider, S. J., Ratisbonae, Neo Eboraci et Cincinnatii, 1885.

Rules of the Third Order Secular of St. Francis:

Original Rule of 1221: *Regula Antiqua Fratrum et Sororum de Paenitentia seu Tertii Ordinis Sancti Francisci . . . edidit P. Sabatier* (*Opuscules de Critique Historique,* I, 17-30, Paris, 1901).

Rule of Nicholas IV in 1289 (*Bull. Rom.*, IV, 90-95; *Bull. Franc.*, IV, n. 150, p. 94-97; *Bull. Franc. Epitome*, p. 302-305; Antonius de Cipressa, *Regula sive Modus Vivendi Tertii Ordinis S. Francisci*, p. 63-81; *Seraphicae Legislationis Textus Originales*, 77-94).

Statutes of Innocent XI, or, *Statuta Innocentiana* (Antonius de Cipressa, *o. c.*, p. 82-122).

Rule of Leo XIII, promulgated in the Const., *Misericors Dei Filius*, May 30, 1883 (*Fontes*, n. 588).

Seraphicae Legislationis Textus Originales, Quaracchi, 1897.

Summarium Indulgentiarum, Privilegiorum et Indultorum a Sede Apostolica O. F. M. Cap. Concessorum, Romae, 1905.

Wadding, Lucas, O. F. M., *Annales Minorum (regestra pontificum)*, 18 vols., Romae, 1731-1736.

II. AUTHORS

A. Ss.-Acta Sanctorum . . . collegit, digessit, illustravit Johannes Bollandus S. J. Godefridus Henschius . . .,54 vols., Antwerp, 1643-1853.

Annales Ordinis Praedicatorum, vol. I, Romae, 1756.

Antonius de Cipressa, O. M. Obs., *Regula sive Modus Vivendi Fratrum de Poenitentia Tertii Ordinis Saecularis S. Francisci*, Romae, 1865.

Auvrey, *Manuel du Tiers Ordre de Premontre*, Caen, 1924.

[Bachofen], Charles Augustine, *A Commentary on the New Code of Canon Law*, 3 ed., 8 vols., New York-St. Louis, 1921-1924.

Bakalarczyk, Richardus, *De Novitiatu*, Washington, D. C., 1927.

Benedicti XIV, *Institutiones Ecclesiasticae*, Prati, 1844.

Beringer, Franz, S. J., *Die Ablässe, ihr Wesen und Gebrauch*, 2 vols., Paderborn, 1921-1922.

Boehmer, H., *Analekten zur Geschichte des Franciscus von Assisi*, Tübigen und Leipsig, 1904.

Bondini, Aloisius, O. M. C., *De Privilegio Exemptionis seu de Regularium Immunitate ab Ordinariorum Jurisdictione*, Romae, 1919.

Brück, *Lehrbuch der Kirchengeschichte*, Mainz, 1902.

Buchberger, *Kirchliches Handlexikon*, 2 vols., Munich, 1907 and 1912.

Callaey, Fredegand, O. M. Cap., *The Third Order of St. Francis* (translated by John Lenhart, O. M. Cap.), Pittsburgh, 1926.

Catholic Encyclopedia, The, vol. XIV, New York, 1914.

Cerri, Giovanni, O. F. M., Il. *Terz' Ordine Francescano*, 2 ed., Roma, 1921.

Chelodi, Joannes, *Jus de Personis*, 2 ed., Tridenti, 1927.

Cocchi, Guidus, *Commentarium in Codicem Juris Canonici*, vols. III and IV, 2 ed., Taurinorum Augustae, 1925-1926.

Currier, *History of Religious Orders,* New York, 1913.

Cuthbert, O. S. F. C., *Life of St. Francis of Assisi,* London, 1925.

Davison, E. S., *Some Forerunners of St. Francis of Assisi,* Columbia University, 1907.

Drane, *The History of St. Dominic,* London, New York, 1891.

Du Cange, Ch., *Glossarium ad Scriptores,* 6 vols., Paris, 1738.

[ ] *English Dominican Province, The,* London, 1921.

Fanfani, Ludovicus, O. P., *De Jure Religiosorum ad norman Codicis Juris Canonici,* Augustae Taurinoru-Romae, 1920.

——, *De Indulgentiis, Manuale Theoretico-Bracticum ad Norman Codicis Juris Canonici,* 2. ed., Taurini-Romae, 1926.

Felder, Hilarin, O. M. Cap., *The Ideals of St. Francis of Assisi* (translated by Berchmans Little, O. M. Cap.), New York, Cincinnati, Chicago, 1925.

Ferraris, F. Lucii, O. M. Reg. Obs., *Biblioteca Canonica, Juridica, Moralis, Theologica necnon Ascetica, Polemica, Rubristica, Hostorica,* 9 vols., Romae, 1885-1892.

Ferreres, Joannes, S. J., *Institutiones Canonicae,* 2 ed., 2 vols., Barcinone, 1920.

Ferreres, Giovanni, S. J., *Le Confraternite e Congregazioni Ecclesiastiche,* Venezia, 1909.

Flaminio di Parma, P., O. M. Obs., *Memorie istoriche delle chiese e conventi dell' Osservante e Reformata Prov di Bologna,* vol I, Parma, 1760.

Frederici, *Istoria de Cavalieri Gaudenti,* 2 vols., Vinegia, 1787.

Gennari, Casimiro Card., *Quistioni Canoniche,* Roma, 1908.

——, *Quistioni Theologico-Morali,* 2 ed., Roma, 1907.

Geudens, *Manual of the Third Order of St. Norbert,* London, 1889.

Grecchio, *Manuale Praelati Franciscani,* Romae, 1862.

Heigl, *Die Weltlichen Oblaten des heilegen Benedictus* (*Studien und Mittheilungen aus dem Benedictiner Orden, II*), Wuerzburg, 1885.

Heimbucher, M., *Die Orden und Kongregationen der katholischen Kirche;* 2 ed., 3 vols., Paderborn, 1907-1908.

Hergenröther-Hanlen, *Welzer und Welte's Kirchenlexikon,* 12 vols., Freiburg, 1882-1901.

Hergenröther, Joseph Card., *Theologische Bibliotek,* vol. II, Freiburg im Breisgau, 1904.

Hilarius Parisiensis, O. M. Cap., *Liber Tertii Ordinis S. Francisci Assisiensis, Paris,* 1888.

Holwerk, F. G., *A Biographical Dictionary of the Saints,* St. Louis and London, 1924.

Holzapfel, Heribert, O. F. M., *Die Leitung des Dritten Ordens,* München, 1925.

Holzapfel, Heribert, O. F. M., *Manuale Historiae O. F. M.*, Freiburg, 1909.

Hugo, Lud. Card., O. Praem., *Sacri et canonici O. Praem. Annales*, 2 vols., Nancaei, 1734-1736.

I Fioretti-Les Petites Fleurs de la petit Pauvre de Jesus-Christ Saint Francis D'Assise, ed. by Goffin, Paris, 10 ed.

Jacobili, L., *Vita della B. Angelina*, Bologna, 1659.

Jöergensen, *St. Francis of Assisi*, London, 1913.

Kirkfleet, Cornelius, O. Praem., *History of St. Norbert*, St. Louis and London, 1916.

Le Paige, Joannes, O. Praem., *Biblioteca Ord. Praemonstratensis*, 2 vols., Parisiis, 1633.

Little, A. G., *A Guide to Franciscan Studies*, London, 1920.

Little, W. J. Knox, *St. Francis of Assisi*, New York, 1897.

Lyszczarczyk, Venantius, O. F. M., *Compendium Privilegiorum Regularium praesertim Ordinis Fratrum Minorum*, Leopoli, 1906.

Mandonnet, R. P., O. P., *Les Origines de L'Ordo de Poenitentia* (*Comte Rendu du Quatrieme Congres Scientifique International des Catholiques-Sciences Historiques*), *183-215*, Freiburg, 1898.

——, *Les Regles et Le Gouvernement de L'Ordo de Poenitentia au XIII Siècle* (*Opuscules de Critique Historique, I, 143-250*, Paris, 1902.

Manual for Secular Oblates of St. Benedict, Beatty, Pa., 1923.

Marianus de Florentia, *Compendium Chronicorum Fratrum Minorum*, Quaracchi, 1911; also published periodically in *A. F. H.*, I-IV.

Maroto, Philippus, *Institutiones Juris Canonici*, 3 ed., vol. I, Romae, 1921.

M. G. H. Ss.,—*Monumenta Germaniae Historica Scriptores*, Vols. XXIII-XXVI, Hannover, 1916.

Mileta, Hieronymus, M., O. M. C., *Enchiridion pro Directoribus Tertii Ordinis Saecularis S. P. Francisci Assisiensis*, Romae, 1913.

Mileta, G. M., O. M. C., *Trattato Giuridico sul Terz' Ordine Secolare di S. Francesco D'Assisi*, Roma, 1921.

Mortier, *Histoire des Maitres Généraux De L'Ordre des Frères Prêcheurs*, Paris, 1905.

Mocchegiani, Petrus, O. F. M., *Collectio Indulgentiarum, theologice, canonice ac historice digesta*, Quaracchi, 1897.

——, *Jurisprudentia Ecclesiastica ad Usum et Commoditatem utriusque Cleri*, 2 vols., Quaracchi, 1905.

Müller, Karl, *Die Anfänge des Minoritenordens und der Bussbruderschaften*, Freiburg, 1885.

Ojetti, Benedictus, S. J., *Synopsis Rerum Moralium et Juris Pontificii*, 3 ed., 4 vols., Romae, 1909-1914.

Parsons, Reuben, *Studies in Church History,* vol. II, 2 ed., New York and Cincinnati, 1906.

Piat, F., Montensis, O. M. Cap., *Praelectiones Juris Regularis,* 2 vols., 3 ed., Tornaci, 1906.

Prümmer, Dominicus, O. P., *Manuale Juris Canonici,* 3 ed., Friburgi Brisgoviae, 1922.

——, *Manuale Juris Ecclesiastici,* vol. II (*Jus Regularium Speciale*), Friburgi Brisgoviae, 1907.

Putzer, Joseph, C. SS. R., *Commentarium in Facultates Apostolicas,* 4 ed., New York, 1897.

Quigley, Joseph, *Condemned Societies,* Washington, D. C., 1927.

Reiffenstuel, F. Anacletus, *Jus Canonicum Universum, clara methodo juxta titulos quinque librorum Decretalium,* 5 vols., Antwerpiae, 1743.

Robinson, Paschal, O. F. M., *The Writings of St. Francis of Assisi,* Philadelphia, 1906.

Sabatier, Paulus, *Actus B. Francisci,* Parisiis, 1902.

S. Bonaventurae Opera Omnia, 10 vols., Quaracchi, 1882-1902.

Stein, Paulus, O. F. M., *Tertius Ordo Franciscalis,* 3 ed., Woerden in Hollandia, 1923.

Tischler, Franz, O. M. Cap., *Handbuch zur Leitung des Dritten Ordens des heiligen Franziskus,* Bregenz am Bodensee, 1912.

Van Den Borne, Fidentius, O. F. M., *Die Anfänge des Franziskanischen Dritten Ordens* (*Franziskanische Studien, Beiheft VIII*), Münster, 1925.

Vermeersch, A., S. J., *De Religiosis Institutis et Personis tractatus canonico-moralis,* 2 ed., vol. I, Romae et Ratisbonae, 1907.

Vermeersch-Creusen—Vermeersch, A., S. J.—Creusen, J., S. J., *Epitome Juris Canonici cum Comentariis ad Scholas et ad Usum privatum,* vol. I, 3 ed., 1927.

Vermeersch, A., S. J., *Periodica de Re Canonical et Morali,* vol. XIII, Romae, 1925.

Wadding, Lucas, O. F. M., *Annales Minorum,* 18 vols., Romae, 1731-1736.

Wernz, Franciscus, X., S. J., *Jus Decretalium,* 2 ed., 6 vols., Romae, 1908.

Works of St. Francis of Assisi, by a Religious of the Order, London, 1882.

III. Periodicals

Analecta Franciscana, Quaracchi, 1885-.

A. F. H.-Archivum Franciscanum Historicum, Quaracchi, 1908-.

Bei St. Franziskus, *Gedanken und Nachrichten aus den Klöstern,*

Veröffentlicht im Auftrage des Provinzialiates zu Fulda, Juli, 1927.
CpR.-Commentarium pro Religiosis, Romae, 1920-.
Franziskanische Studien, Beiheft VIII, Münster, 1925.
Revue Bènèdictine, vol. III, abbaye de Maredsous, Belgique, 1886-1887.
Month, The, London, 1864-.
Third Order Rorum, The, Chicago, 1922-.

Universitas Catholica Americae

WASHINGTONII, D. C.

FACULTAS JURIS CANONICI

1927-1928

No. 50

DEUS LUX MEA

THESES

QUAS

AD DOCTORATUS GRADUM

IN JURE CANONICO

APUD UNIVERSITATEM CATHOLICAM AMERICAE

CONSEQUENDUM

PUBLICE PROPUGNABIT

GERALDUS JOSEPHUS REINMANN

SACERDOS EX ORDINE FRATRUM MINORUM CONVENTUALIUM

BACCALAUREUS ARTIUM

ET

LICENTIATUS IN JURE CANONICO

HORA IX A. M. DIE II JUNII A. D. MCMXXVIII

JUS CANONICUM

I.	De Relatione inter Ecclesiam et Statum	
II.	De Dissertatione	
III.	De Historia Juris Canonici	
IV.	De Ambitu Codicis	Canones 1-7
V.	De Legibus Ecclesiasticis	Canones 8-24
VI.	De Consuetudine	Canones 25-30
VII.	De Temporis Supputatione	Canones 31-35
VIII.	De Rescriptis	Canones 36-63
IX.	De Privilegiis	Canones 63-79
X.	De Dispensatione	Canones 80-86
XI.	De Synodo Dioecesana	Canones 356-362
XII.	De Curia Dioecesana	Canones 363-390
XIII.	De Consultoribus Dioecesanis	Canones 423-428
XIV.	De Parochis et Vicariis Paroecialibus	Canones 451-478
XV.	De Ecclesiarum Rectoribus	Canones 479-486
XVI.	De Simonia	Canones 726-730
XVII.	De Ministro et Subjecto Sacrae Ordinationis	Canones 951-991
XVIII.	De iis quae Matrimonii Celebrationi praemitti debent	Canones 1019-1034
XIX.	De Impedimentis Matrimonialibus	Canones 1035-1080
XX.	De Consensu Matrimoniali	Canones 1081-1093
XXI.	De Forma Celebrationis Matrimonii	Canones 1094-1107
XXII.	De Tempore et Loco Celebrationis Matrimonii	Canones 1108-1109
XXIII.	De Matrimonii Effectibus	Canones 1110-1117
XXIV.	De Separatione Conjugum	Canones 1118-1132
XXV.	De Matrimonii Convalidatione	Canones 1133-1141
XXVI.	De Foro Competenti	Canones 1556-1568
XXVII.	De Tribunali Ordinario Primae Instantiae	Canones 1572-1593

XXVIII.	De Tribunali Ordinario Secundae Instantiae	Canones 1594-1596
XXIX.	De Ordinariis Apostolicae Sedis Tribunalibus	Canones 1597-1605
XXX.	De Officio Judicum et Tribunalis Ministrorum	Canones 1608-1626
XXXI.	De Ordine Cognitionum	Canones 1627-1633
XXXII.	De Personis ad Disceptationem Judicialem Admittendis et de Modo Confectionis et Conservationis Actorum	Canones 1640-1645
XXXIII.	De Partibus in Causa	Canones 1646-1666
XXXIV.	De Actionibus et Exceptionibus	Canones 1667-1705
XXXV.	De Causae Introductione	Canones 1706-1725
XXXVI.	De Litis Contestatione	Canones 1726-1731
XXXVII.	De Litis Instantia	Canones 1732-1741
XXXVIII.	De Interrogationibus Partibus in Judicio Faciendis	Canones 1742-1746
XXXIX.	De Probationibus	Canones 1747-1769
XL.	De Causis Matrimonialibus	Canones 1960-1992
XLI.	De Causis contra Sacram Ordinationem	Canones 1993-1998
XLII.	De Remotione et Translatione Parochorum	Canones 2147-2167
XLIII.	De Modo Procedendi contra Clericos non Residentes, contra Clericos Concubinarios et contra Parochum Negligentem	Canones 2168-2185
XLIV.	De Modo Procedendi in Suspensione ex Informata Conscientia Infligenda	Canones 2186-2194
XLV.	De Poenis et Censuris in Genere	Canones 2214-2254

ROMAN LAW

XLVI. Periods of Roman Law
XLVII. Personality
XLVIII. Citizenship
XLIX. The Roman Family
L. *Cura* and *Tutela*
LI. Adoption
LII. Roman Marriage
LIII. Modes of Acquiring Singular Things
LIV. Modes of Acquiring an Aggregate of Things

Vidit Facultas Juris Canonici:
PHILIPPUS BERNARDINI, S. T. D., J. U. D., *Decanus*
LUDOVICUS MOTRY, S. T. D., J. C. D., *a Secretis*
VALENTINUS SCHAAF, O. F. M., S. T. B., J. C. D.
FRANCISCUS LARDONE, S. T. D., J. U. D.

Vidit Rector Universitatis:
THOMAS J. SHAHAN, S. T. D., J. U. D.

BIOGRAPHICAL NOTE

Joseph Anthony Reinmann was born in Syracuse, New York, July 25, 1902. After completing his elementary and secondary education, he entered the novitiate of the Order of Friars Minor Conventual, taking the name of Gerald Joseph Reinmann. He was professed in the Order August 4, 1921, and entered the Seminary of the Order at St.-Anthony-on-Hudson, Rensselaer, New York, in the fall of that year, where he was ordained to the Holy Priesthood, May 30, 1926. The following September he entered the graduate School of Canon Law at the Catholic University of America.

www.ingramcontent.com/pod-product-compliance
Lightning Source LLC
LaVergne TN
LVHW050238080826
844660LV00012B/551

9780813222394